SEVEN TOOLS

FOR BUILDING EFFECTIVE GROUPS

A PILGRIMAGE
SMALL GROUP GUIDE BY
JEFFREY ARNOLD

D1024177

NAVPRESS
BRINGING TRUTH TO LIFE
NavPress Publishing Group
P.O. Box 35001, Colorado Springs, Colorado 80935

OUR GUARANTEE TO YOU

We believe so strongly in the message of our books that we are making this quality guarantee to you. If for any reason you are disappointed with the content of this book, return the title page to us with your name and address and we will refund to you the list price of the book. To help us serve you better, please briefly describe why you were disappointed. Mail your refund request to: NavPress, P.O. Box 35002, Colorado Springs, CO 80935.

The Navigators is an international Christian organization. Our mission is to reach, disciple, and equip people to know Christ and to make Him known through successive generations. We envision multitudes of diverse people in the United States and every other nation who have a passionate love for Christ, live a lifestyle of sharing Christ's love, and multiply spiritual laborers among those without Christ.

NavPress is the publishing ministry of The Navigators. NavPress publications help believers learn biblical truth and apply what they learn to their lives and ministries. Our mission is to stimulate spiritual formation among our readers.

Cover photo: Steve Eames

Pilgrimage small group study guides are published in conjunction with The Pilgrimage Group, an organization that trains pastors and lay leaders across the United States and Canada in the essentials of small group ministry and leadership. For more information on Pilgrimage training or consulting, call 1-800-477-7787. Or, visit the Pilgrimage web site at http//www.pilgrimage.org/training/.

Unless otherwise identified, all Scripture quotations in this publication are taken from the *HOLY BIBLE: NEW INTERNATIONAL VERSION* ® (NIV®). Copyright © 1973, 1978, 1984 by International Bible Society, used by permission of Zondervan Publishing House, all rights reserved. The other version used is *The Message* (MSG) by Eugene H. Peterson, copyright © 1993, 1994, 1995, 1996, used by permission of NavPress Publishing Group.

Printed in the United States of America

2 3 4 5 6 7 8 9 10 11 12 13 14 15 / 05 04 03 02 01

Contents

How This Study Guide Works

▼ ▼ ▼ ▼ ▼ ▼ ▼ ▼ ▼ ▼ ▼ ▼ ▼ ▼ ▼ ▼ ▼ ▼ ▼ ▼
Equipping Leaders

What is effective leadership?

Countless books have been written about it. Numerous lectures and seminars offer perspectives on it. Colleges and seminaries prepare people for it. And yet, few really feel equipped to lead effectively.

Leadership is not some facilitative technique in which a super-understanding person listens. Nor is it an authoritative barking of commands by a military-style boss. It is not fully personified by a "coach" who teaches people to work together for a common goal. And it is not totally exemplified by a professorial teacher who covers all angles in complete lecture format.

Leadership includes those styles, but is much more than any one of them. It is best represented as a tool kit from which skills and techniques are pulled at appropriate times. Those who lead must constantly learn new skills and hone older ones. They must continuously challenge themselves to new levels of understanding, insight, and effectiveness. They must diligently pursue Christlike character and Christ-taught wisdom.

The people of God need leaders who are willing to grow, no matter what level they have attained. The purpose of this resource is to equip leaders with new levels of understanding and skill. This guide was designed primarily with small group leaders in mind, but also works well as a training tool for:

► apprentices
► Sunday school teachers
► youth ministry leaders
► college ministry leaders

5

- children's ministry leaders
- committees
- ministry teams

This resource offers growing leaders an opportunity to partner together in an exciting, relational, hands-on learning approach. By using a small-group format, group members will:

- encourage one another to learn about and use several key leadership tools
- engage in individual and group reflection
- receive individual analysis of their skills
- participate in creative Bible study and group process
- work together to solve intriguing leadership problems
- learn to receive care from other leaders
- create a structured small group for continued leadership support and prayer
- practice daily disciplines necessary to grow as a leader

Why These Tools?

When preparing to write this resource, I culled leadership books (some of them appear at the end of various sessions in the resource lists) and made extensive lists. I omitted tools that were either redundant or otherwise closely associated with others on the list. While it would be easy to generate a list of more than seven tools that leaders need, I have found these to be the primary ones I have needed as a pastor and the most useful to leaders whom I train.

NavPress/Pilgrimage has published a companion resource to this one entitled *Seven Traits of a Successful Leader*. These resources are designed to help leaders study leadership issues prayerfully in an interactive group environment, in such a way that both God's work (traits) and ours (tools) are emphasized.

Building Community

The life of following Christ was never meant to be solitary. The early Christians pursued it in groups not much larger than your small group. They met exclusively in homes for the first two hundred years or so of the movement. By meeting in a small group, you are imitating a time-tested format for spiritual life.

People join small groups for all sorts of reasons: to get to know a few people well; to be cared for; to learn; to grow spiritually. We believe small groups are the ideal setting in which people can learn what it means to take on the character of Christ and practice the process of becoming like Christ. While there are many spiritually helpful things one can do alone or in a large group, a small group offers many advantages. Among other things, group members can:

- ► encourage one another in good times and bad
- ► ask thoughtful questions when a member has a decision to make
- ► listen to God together
- ► pray for each other
- ► benefit from one another's insights into the Scripture
- ► acquire a habit of reading the Bible on a regular basis
- ► practice loving their neighbors
- ► worship God together
- ► learn to communicate effectively
- ► solve problems together
- ► learn to receive care from others
- ► experience the pleasure of helping another person grow

This study guide emphasizes skill development and relationship building. It will help you explore what it means to be an effective leader among the people of God. You will engage in reflection, study, interaction, problem solving, and prayer. You will be challenged to adopt personal homework electives so that you can continue exploring leadership tools during the week. You will identify who you are as a leader and what you need to work on. You will draw closer to people who can continue to support you as a leader after the group is over.

A Modular Approach

Each session is divided into several modules or sections. Times are suggested for each module so that you can complete the session in 60 to 90 minutes. The core modules include:

Overview: The first page of each session describes the objectives for your meeting so that you will know what to expect and what results to strive for. You will also learn something about the author's own story as it relates to the topic at hand.

Beginning: Building relationships is a necessary part of each group experience. Each session will have several questions to help you learn who the other members are and where they have been in their lives. The beginning questions also help you begin thinking about a particular leadership issue in preparation for a time of Bible study and problem solving.

The Text: Studying a biblical text is an integral part of this guide. You will examine brief passages from various parts of the Bible. *THE MESSAGE* by Eugene Peterson and *THE NEW INTERNATIONAL VERSION* have been chosen where appropriate. *THE MESSAGE* is deliberately relational and will help those familiar with Scripture to see certain passages with new eyes. Since the New Testament was written to be read aloud, you will begin your study by reading the text aloud. Words in bold type are explained in the Reference Notes section.

Understanding the Text: Unless you notice carefully what the text says, you will not be able to interpret it accurately. The questions in this section will help you focus on the key issues and wrestle with what the text means. In this section you will concentrate on the passage in its original first-century context.

Applying the Text: It is not enough to simply understand the passage; you need to apply that understanding to your situation. The questions in this section connect what you have read to how you should live. This section will encourage you to do problem solving and creative application of leadership tools.

Assignment: To allow for flexibility with groups as well as individuals, this guide offers homework electives. There is a reflection elective to encourage you to identify where you are as a leader, and where you need to begin work. There is also a project elective with simple tasks for you to perform. You may decide to let each person in the group choose the homework he or she prefers, since people's personalities differ. However, there is a greater chance that people will actually do the homework if everyone does the same thing and can compare results than if everyone does something different. Hence, you may decide to agree on the same homework elective each week. It's best to be honest with one another about what homework one can reasonably commit to.

Prayer: Praying together can be one of the most faith-building and relationship-building things you do together. Suggestions are made to facilitate this time in the group.

Reference Notes: In order to accurately understand the meaning of the text, one needs to know a little about the context in which it was written and the key words and phrases it contains. The notes include background on the characters, information about cultural practices, word definitions, and so on. You will find entries in this section for those words and phrases in the text that are printed in bold type. You can scan the notes after reading the text aloud, or during your discussion of Understanding the Text.

Additional Resources: A few suggestions will be offered for further reading in relation to the topic at hand. At times, a quotation will be provided.

Help for the Leader

This guide provides everything the leader needs to facilitate the group's discussion. In each session, the ❶ symbol designates instructions for the leader. Since this group is for leaders, you may consider taking turns facilitating the discussion. Or, the official leader may want to delegate certain responsibilities, such as leading prayer, worship, or discussion.

Answers to Common Questions

Who is this material designed for?

▶ Any persons who want to challenge themselves to more effective leadership in a church context, especially leaders of small groups.
▶ Leaders who want the support that a small group offers.

How often should we meet?

▶ Once a week is best; every other week works as well; and some churches will encourage their leaders to use this resource once per month.

How long should we meet?

▶ If you abbreviate some sections, you will need at least an hour.
▶ Ninety minutes is best—this gives time for more discussion.
▶ Some groups may want to meet for two hours, especially if you have more than eight people.

What if we only have 50 minutes?

> ▶ Cut back on the Beginning section and adapt the
> Applying the Text problem solvers. Read the text
> quickly and pray only briefly.

Is homework necessary?

> ▶ No, the group can meet with no prior preparation.
> ▶ The Assignments, especially the project and reflection,
> will greatly increase what you gain from the group.

Reflective Listening

▼ ▼ ▼ ▼ ▼ ▼ ▼ ▼ ▼ ▼ ▼ ▼ ▼ ▼ ▼ ▼ ▼ ▼ ▼
Overview   10 minutes

❶ *Make sure that everybody has been welcomed to the group and that the room is comfortably arranged. If leaders do not know each other, exchange names.*
If they do not know you, introduce yourself to the group, sharing:

> ► *your name*
> ► *your leadership role*
> ► *several objectives you have for this leadership group*

If there are others sharing leadership responsibility with you, perhaps a host or hostess, introduce them as well.
Then, briefly sketch out your agenda for the meeting. What should leaders-in-training expect to happen? Pass out discussion guides if necessary. Ask someone to read aloud this story and the objectives that follow.

I was having a hard day. Actually, I was having a difficult month. I was in one of those valleys Christians find themselves in when God is deepening their faith. God may have been working in my life, but I was not happy with the by-products: frustration and a feeling of being overwhelmed.

On this particular day, one of my church friends with lots of problems chose to visit. She wanted to talk about her life and the troubles she was encountering. I had heard it all many times before. Somehow she never seemed to get past her problems, and I was tired of listening to her.

So I told her my problems. Actually, I did let her begin to talk. I just got tired of listening and, when I found an appropriate spot, I jumped in with one of those I-know-just-what-you're-going-through phrases. It worked. I dumped, she listened, and then she left.

After she left I had a vague sense that something had not gone well. That night as I reflected on my day, I realized I had made some big mistakes. First, I treated her as others had for years: listen; pay as little attention as possible; pray that she leaves in a reasonable amount of time; and get on with my life. Instead of listening to what she was saying, I allowed her words to bounce off someone yet another time. Second, I used her by telling her my own problems, something best saved for those who could truly help me, including God. Third, I was again reminded that I have a difficult time listening, not just to others but also to myself.

Listening is a difficult skill to cultivate, yet it is also foundational to who we are as God's people. Genesis 1:27 says that we are made in God's image. The interesting thing about an "image" is that it is a reflection. We don't just mirror God's image to ourselves as if in a vacuum. We interact as God's people, "reflecting" together on what it means to be God's children and the family of faith. We are to listen to one another, to ourselves, and to God in community. To function best in community, God's leaders must learn to be reflective listeners.

In this session we will:

► discuss the concept of reflective listening
► examine what Scripture says about reflective listening
► begin to develop the skill of reflective listening

▼ ▼ ▼ ▼ ▼ ▼ ▼ ▼ ▼ ▼ ▼ ▼ ▼ ▼ ▼ ▼ ▼ ▼ ▼
Beginning   15 minutes

❶ *Read aloud this explanation of sharing questions.*

Sharing our stories allows us to begin listening to each other. We earn each other's trust by giving and receiving our stories.

As the group grows in trust, you will more effectively begin to interact with each other and reflect on what individuals are sharing.

Go around the room and allow each person to answer the first question before moving to the next one. The leader should go first each time.

1. When you were disciplined as a child, how did you typically respond?

    ❐ ignore them—maybe they'll go away
    ❐ fight them—maybe they'll get tired and give up
    ❐ apologize—maybe they'll finish up more quickly
    ❐ blame others—maybe they'll be sidetracked
    ❐ cry—maybe they'll feel sorry for me and go easy on the punishment
    ❐ other:

2. Think of one person in your life who was or is a consistently poor listener.

    ❐ Who is the person?
    ❐ What did that person do that made you not feel heard?

3. Think of one person in your life who was or is a consistently good listener.

    ❐ Who is the person?
    ❐ What gives you the sense that this person really listens?

▼ ▼ ▼ ▼ ▼ ▼ ▼ ▼ ▼ ▼ ▼ ▼ ▼ ▼ ▼ ▼ ▼ ▼ ▼
The Text   5 minutes

The book of James is one of the most practical books in the Bible. Its key thought is that "faith . . . not accompanied by action, is dead" (see James 2:14-17). The primary focus is on some of the areas of life that faith affects. Our passage examines the relationship between listening, reflecting, and doing.

❶ *Have someone read the text aloud. You may also read some or all of the reference notes on pages 20-21.*

Post this at all the intersections, dear friends: Lead with your ears, follow up with your tongue, and let anger straggle along in the rear. **God's righteousness doesn't grow from human anger.** So throw all spoiled virtue and cancerous evil in the garbage. In simple **humility**, let our gardener, God, landscape you with the Word, **making a salvation-garden of your life.**

Don't fool yourself into thinking that you are a listener when you are anything but, letting the Word go in one ear and out the other. *Act* on what you hear! Those who hear and don't act are like those **who glance in the mirror,** walk away, and two minutes later have no idea who they are, what they look like. But whoever catches a glimpse of the revealed counsel of God—the free life!—even out of the corner of his eye, and sticks with it, is no distracted scatterbrain but a man or woman of action. That person will find delight and affirmation in the action.

Anyone who sets himself up as "religious" by talking a good game is self-deceived. This kind of religion is **hot air and only hot air.** Real religion, the kind that passes muster before God the Father, is this: Reach out to the homeless and loveless in their plight, and guard against corruption from the godless world.

(James 1:19-27, MSG)

Understanding the Text   20 minutes

4. What does it mean, at the beginning of the passage, that we are to lead with our ears and follow up with our tongue?

5. Woven through this passage is a detailed contrast between a godly person who listens and a reactive person whose life is inconsistent. Make note of all the references to each. How does the image of the mirror explain the difference between the two individuals?

6. There are two dimensions of listening highlighted in this passage.

   a. First is our interpersonal relationships with one another. Locate all references in this passage that indicate how we are to listen to one another. How would you summarize them?

   b. Second is our listening to God. Locate all references in this passage that indicate how we are to listen to God. How would you summarize them?

Applying the Text   20 minutes

We can derive several principles of reflective listening from our text:

► Reflective listening requires persistent attempts to understand (verses 19-21).
► Reflective listening requires persistent attempts to discern God's will and way (verses 22-25).
► Reflective listening requires a humble understanding of one's own shortcomings (verses 21,26).
► Reflective listening produces fruit not in words but in action (verses 26-27).

7. a. Of the four principles just listed, which do you do well?

    b. Which do you need to develop better?

If these are qualities of effective leaders, we can say, by contrast, that according to this passage, ineffective leaders are:

► quick to act without fully understanding
► stubborn or rebellious
► prideful or headstrong
► inconsistent

8. To what degree are any of these attributes true of you?

9. Respond to the following situations by:
    ❏ identifying how people normally respond to such situations
    ❏ deciding how an effective leader applies good listening skills in such situations

    a. A person calls you and says that people in the church are talking about how you do not come prepared to lead your group or class.

16

b. While listening to a sermon, it occurs to you that the person sitting next to you needs just the kind of "spiritual help" the pastor is preaching about.

c. A friend of yours is extremely insensitive to his wife and doesn't seem willing to grow in his faith. You are mad at him, and are praying about him.

d. You have felt distant from God for a long time, and unable to pray. You wonder why God has removed Himself from you.

10. Reflectively listen to your group, allowing people to respond to these questions as they feel led:

❏ How do I feel about our meeting time today?
❏ What are my concerns or fears as this group begins working through this resource?
❏ What positive and negative aspects of listening have occurred in this group during this discussion?

11. Read the sections EQUIPPING LEADERS and BUILDING COMMUNITY on pages 5-7.

a. What aspects of those sections are most attractive to you?

b. Does anything in them confuse or trouble you?
Explain.

12. Read through the following list of ground rules for being
in this leaders' group. Discuss how each ground rule will
help the group to be a listening group. Add or adapt them
as best suits your group.

❒ Affirm one another's contributions—practice
acceptance
❒ What is spoken in the group remains in the group—
practice confidentiality
❒ As you are able, be honest and forthright with one
another—practice openness
❒ Do not speak about a person when he or she is not
present—practice graciousness
❒ When the group agrees to homework, come
prepared—practice self-discipline
❒ When the group meets, come on time—practice
courtesy
❒ Do not monopolize time so that others can speak—
practice listening

▼ ▼ ▼ ▼ ▼ ▼ ▼ ▼ ▼ ▼ ▼ ▼ ▼ ▼ ▼ ▼ ▼ ▼
Assignment   10 minutes

Decide which of the following homework electives each of you
will do. Make sure that your choices are reasonable and will be
performed by everyone prior to the next meeting.

Elective 1: Reflection—Begin a journal, which you will keep
during the next seven weeks and hopefully continue after the
course is done. Purchase a notebook and put your name on the
outside. For this week's reflection, put a heading like "Reflective
Listening" at the top of the first page. Spend about half an hour
writing your answers to the following questions. Consider sharing the results with a person who is close to you:

- What is one example of an unresolved conflict or hurt in my life? What in my life keeps me from hearing and reconciling with difficult situations or persons?

- How would I rate my ability to listen to the following persons: my spouse; my child(ren); my family; my neighbors; my friends; my work associates?

- Of the relationships contained in the previous question, what are two that I need to work on, and what are steps I can take to become a more reflective, listening person?

- Make a "brainstorm" list of the following:

  a. all possible words that describe your listening ability.
  b. all possible words that you wish described your listening ability.
  c. at least two or three from your "wish" list that you will work on.

Elective 2: Project—It is often easier to perceive weaknesses in others than in ourselves. This assignment involves locating others' weaknesses and your own.

- Before the next meeting, observe *at least* five instances in which others applied poor listening techniques. Be prepared to share at least one of the conversations.

- Also, observe *at least* five instances in your own conversation when you applied poor listening techniques. Be prepared to share at least one of the conversations.

▼ ▼ ▼ ▼ ▼ ▼ ▼ ▼ ▼ ▼ ▼ ▼ ▼ ▼ ▼ ▼ ▼ ▼
Prayer   5 minutes

Stand in a circle. Briefly allow each person to finish this statement: "One thing I would like God to do in my life based on this session is. . . ." Hold hands if you are comfortable doing so. Let each person pray aloud, beginning with the leader. Consider praying by name for the people in your group, listing the requests that they shared. If you would rather pray silently, please say "Amen" aloud to let the other people know you are finished.

▼ ▼ ▼ ▼ ▼ ▼ ▼ ▼ ▼ ▼ ▼ ▼ ▼ ▼ ▼ ▼ ▼ ▼ ▼
Reference Notes

Setting: The letter of James was most likely written by James, the brother of Jesus. He was an early leader in the Jerusalem church, and his letter is written from a Jewish perspective. James wrote to Jews scattered by persecution throughout the Roman world. He was concerned not with how people came to faith in Christ (faith was assumed), but with how they lived out that faith in a sinful world. One of the themes of this book is the tongue; another significant theme is the relationship between faith and life, hearing and doing. Both the tongue and faith/life are addressed in this passage.

Post this at all the intersections, dear friends: James uses a single Greek word (*Iste:* "Listen!"), spoken emphatically, to get his reader's attention. It is a slick attention-getting technique to begin a section on listening with its key word.

God's righteousness doesn't grow from human anger: The common phrase "righteous indignation" presumes that Christians can be angry about certain things, just as God is. While that presumption is not entirely false, there is much danger in it. Human anger is at best a complicated mix including fear, denial, and the justice of our cause. Reactive human anger produces resentment, bitterness, judgment, retaliation, and bruised egos. God's life does not flow from such reactions. But then, can we become angry? Of course. Humans have feelings, and anger is a feeling. We need to understand what is happening not just with others, but inside ourselves. Ephesians 4:26 says, "'In your anger [it is okay to be angry!] do not sin': Do not let the sun go down while you are still angry. . . ." How do we do that? First, we understand our anger. Then, we find a way to reconcile with the person(s) who has offended us. Even if that fails, we must forgive, renouncing the right to nurse rage or seek revenge.

humility: Leaders are often tempted to have a word for each occasion. Thus, they learn to be "quick to speak." However, true leadership begins with humility. A humble person learns through practice to listen and be reflective (slow to speak), patient (not angry), and obedient (see James 1:19, NIV).

making a salvation-garden of your life: James employs an image here of a planted seed. Ridding ourselves of the weeds of wicked-

20

ness and excess (1:21) allows the Word of God humbly received to begin its life-changing work.

who glance in the mirror: The verbs "observes" and "forgets" are in the Greek aorist, and the verb "goes away" is a Greek perfect tense. The effect of the verb differences is illustrated by understanding that a person observes his or her face in the mirror and forgets in one quick moment, but walks away for a lifetime.

hot air and only hot air: Many teachers can speak. It is a wise leader, however, who has control of his or her speech. Our words mean much more than just proving how religious we are—they show the depth of our faith, the conviction of our lives, and the direction of our actions.

Additional Resources

1. David Mains and Melissa Mains Timberlake. *Getting Beyond "How Are You?"*. Wheaton, Ill.: Victor, 1992.

2. William Miller and Kathleen Jackson. *Practical Psychology for Pastors*. Englewood Cliffs, N.J.: Prentice-Hall,1985, chapters 1-5.

Food for Thought

"There is seldom a period in which we do not know what to do, and we move through life in such a distracted way that we do not even take the time and rest to wonder if any of the things we think, say, or do are worth thinking, saying, or doing. We simply go along with the many 'musts' and 'oughts' that have been handed on to us, and we live with them as if they were authentic translations of the Gospel of our Lord. People must be motivated to come to church, youth must be entertained, money must be raised, and above all everyone must be happy. Moreover, we ought to be on good terms with the church and civil authorities; we ought to be liked or at least respected by a fair majority of our parishioners; we ought to move up in the ranks according to schedule; and we ought to have enough vacation and salary to live a comfortable life. . . .

"'Compulsive' is indeed the best adjective for the false self. It points to the need for ongoing and increasing affirmation. Who am I? I am the one who is liked, praised, admired, disliked, hated or despised. Whether I am a pianist, a businessman or a minister, what matters is how I am perceived by my world. . . . These very compulsions are at the basis of the two main enemies of the spiritual life: anger and greed. They are the inner side of a secular life, the sour fruits of our worldly dependencies. What else is anger than the impulsive response to the experience of being deprived? When my sense of self depends on what others say of me, anger is a quite natural reaction to a critical word."

Henri J.M. Nouwen,
The Way of the Heart,
(San Francisco: HarperSanFrancisco, 1981),
pp. 21-23.

Building Healthy Boundaries

Overview ▼▼▼▼▼▼▼▼▼▼▼▼▼▼▼▼▼▼ 10 minutes

❶ *Make sure that any newcomers are introduced and given the appropriate materials. Exchange names if group members' memories need to be refreshed.*

Allow several group members to share what they learned from their homework (if the group did not do homework, encourage members to recap what they learned from the last session). Then ask someone to read aloud this story and the objectives that follow.

There are always several agendas at work whenever Christians gather. There is the Wherever-two-or-more-are-gathered-together-in-my-name agenda. This agenda seeks to do God's will. Then, there is the What-are-we-doing-tonight? agenda. This agenda seeks to accomplish the purpose of the gathering.

There is a secret, unspoken agenda present as well: the What-am-I-doing-here? agenda. Through this agenda people attempt to meet their own wants and needs. Although difficult at first to pinpoint, this agenda becomes more obvious the longer the group meets: Bert has to feel important; Ben fears intimacy; Scott says whatever it takes to be accepted; Jerry is task-oriented and dislikes sharing and community-building; Barbara must always be right.

Because of these agendas, people often feel used or misunderstood. Differences become accentuated. People feel unfulfilled. Groups become lethargic. Early excitement is put aside. Christian mission moves beyond our grasp.

There are two ways to address these unspoken, conflict-laden agendas. The first is to equip leaders and then members to construct healthy boundaries (the subject of this session). The second is to create thorough contracts or covenants whenever Christians get together (the subject of our next session).

Healthy boundaries define agendas. They protect personal space. They create an atmosphere of honesty and accountability. They help us obey the eighth commandment: *Thou shalt not steal* the time, energy, will, space, emotions, and friendship of other group members and leaders.

Boundary building is a skill that allows effective leaders to identify and address unspoken agendas. In this session we will:

> ► define boundaries and discuss how to build them
> ► examine what Scripture has to say about boundaries
> ► begin to identify personal issues that make boundary building difficult

▼ ▼ ▼ ▼ ▼ ▼ ▼ ▼ ▼ ▼ ▼ ▼ ▼ ▼ ▼ ▼ ▼ ▼ ▼
Beginning   10 minutes

❶ *Go around the room and allow each person to answer the first question before moving to the next one. The leader should answer first each time.*

1. Describe a funny practical joke that you either:

   ❐ played on somebody
   ❐ witnessed or heard about
   ❐ had played on you

2. Choose at least one of the following things that makes you uncomfortable, and explain why it does:

   ❐ when a person of the opposite sex gets too close to me physically
   ❐ when a person tries to be my friend too quickly
   ❐ when a person constantly complains about life but never takes my advice

❑ when a person continuously phones me late (too late!) at night "just to chat"

❑ when a person wants to be with me just because of my position and/or title

3. This is a role play. Choose two pairs of people and allow each pair to choose which of the following two situations to act out. Give the pairs a minute to agree on which character each person will play and to read through the script silently. Then let the first team perform for the group, reading the script until it ends and then continuing the conversation on their own. The second team should immediately follow; then you can debrief as a group.

Situation #1:

Characters: A well-meaning but obviously uncomfortable small-group leader; a very needy individual who is a member of the leader's group.

Instructions: Start off reading from the script ($L=$ Leader; $N=$ Needy Individual), then keep going on your own. Both individuals, seated, may pretend that they have a phone to their ears.

Situation: The needy individual has just wakened the leader at midnight with a phone call.

Script:

L: (sleepy) Hello?

N: Hello, _____? This is _____. Did I wake you?

L: (trying to be polite) Well, yes . . .

N: I'm sorry. It's just that—I don't know. I'm having a hard time.

L: With what?

N: I'm feeling like, "What's the use?" You know what I mean?

L: I'm not sure.

N: I don't know you that well, but I feel like we've been friends forever. You're so understanding. It's like we've known each other for a long time. . . .

L: (continue conversation)

25

Situation #2:

Characters: A well-meaning leader, tired after a meeting; an individual who always wants to talk after the meeting.

Situation: The leader has been edging toward the door, preparing to leave after the meeting. The individual moves assertively over and begins the conversation.

Instructions: Start off reading from the script (*L*=Leader; *I*=Individual), then keep going on your own. Both people need to be standing.

Script:

I: Do you have a minute?

L: (shuffles feet uncomfortably) Yes, a moment.

I: You know what I was talking about in our group, with my boss giving me such a hard time and all?

L: Yes, I really felt badly for you.

I: I think she's got it in for me. She never liked me. (*I* moves closer to *L*) I think it's because I don't bow and scrape every time she comes near me.

L: (not sure of what to say, and uncomfortable that *I* has moved closer) Yes.

I: (speaking to the final group members who are leaving) Yes, good night everyone! Say, I've got nowhere to go right now. Let's go grab a cup of coffee, just catch up a little bit. What do you say?

L: I don't know, I really should . . .

I: You know, you're always there for me, and I appreciate that. Thank you. . . . (continue conversation)

4. a. How did the participants feel as they acted out the role play?

   b. How did the observers feel as the situations unfolded in the role play?

Worship
▼▼▼▼▼▼▼▼▼▼▼▼▼▼▼▼▼▼▼▼
10 minutes—Optional

This is a great time to worship as a group if it fits your plan for the group. See the worship section in the appendix. Specific worship suggestions will be provided in later sessions.

The Text
▼▼▼▼▼▼▼▼▼▼▼▼▼▼▼▼▼▼▼
5 minutes

The temptation of Christ is perhaps the most significant passage in Scripture dealing with beneath-the-surface agendas and boundary building. In this story, the temptations represent Satan's agenda and Christ's response delineates His boundaries. There are several ways to look at the three temptations: ways in which Christ was tempted; ways in which we are tempted individually; ways that we are tempted as the community of faith; and ways in which we are tempted as leaders.

❶ *Have someone read the text aloud. You may also read some or all of the reference notes on pages 33-34.*

Next Jesus was taken into the wild by the Spirit for **the Test.** The Devil was ready to give it. Jesus prepared for the Test by fasting forty days and forty nights. That left him, of course, in a state of extreme hunger, which the Devil took advantage of in the first test: "**Since you are God's Son,** speak the word that will turn these stones into loaves of bread."

Jesus answered by quoting Deuteronomy: "**It takes more than bread to stay alive.** It takes a steady stream of words from God's mouth."

For the second test the Devil took him to the Holy City. He sat him on top of the Temple and said, "Since you are God's Son, jump." The Devil goaded him by quoting Psalm 91: "He has placed you in the care of angels. They will catch you so that you won't so much as stub your toe on a stone."

Jesus countered with another citation from Deuteronomy:

"Don't you dare test the Lord your God."

For the third test, the Devil took him on the peak of a huge mountain. He gestured expansively, pointing out all the earth's kingdoms, how glorious they all were. Then he said, "They're yours—lock, stock, and barrel. Just go down on your knees and worship me, and they're yours."

Jesus' refusal was curt: "Beat it, Satan!" He backed his rebuke with a third quotation from Deuteronomy: **"Worship the Lord your God**, and only him. Serve him with absolute single-heartedness."

The Test was over. The Devil left. And in his place, angels! **Angels came** and took care of Jesus' needs.

(Matthew 4:1-11, MSG)

▼ ▼ ▼ ▼ ▼ ▼ ▼ ▼ ▼ ▼ ▼ ▼ ▼ ▼ ▼ ▼ ▼ ▼

Understanding the Text   20 minutes

5. Why do you think Jesus had to undergo "the Test"?

6. Look closely at the first temptation (to turn stones into bread). There seems nothing wrong with Satan's request— after all, Jesus had the power and He was hungry.

   a. What was Satan's agenda?

   b. How did Christ respond to Satan's agenda?

7. Look closely at the second temptation (to jump from the

temple). Although Satan was twisting Scripture, God's angels were protecting Christ.

    a. What was Satan's agenda?

    b. How did Christ respond to his agenda?

8. Look at the third temptation (to bow down to Satan). This one was not subtle at all.

    a. Why might Christ be tempted to bow down to Satan, in as much as these events marked the beginning of Christ's ministry?

    b. What was Satan's agenda with the third temptation?

    c. How did Christ respond to his agenda?

9. First John 2:16 calls the three temptations the "cravings of sinful man, the lust of his eyes and the boasting of what he has and does."

    Malcolm Muggeridge describes the temptations in terms of Jesus' messiahship: A People's Messiah turning stones into bread; a Law Messiah standing on the pinnacle of the Temple; A King Messiah ruling over the whole world.

    Dostoyevsky discusses the temptations in light of the church's sinful use of "miracles, mystery, and authority" (to create, to impress, to coerce).

No matter how you examine the temptations, they are an attempt to short-circuit God's work. Jesus' response to each temptation was boundary building—He defined who He was, who God was to Him, and how He would do ministry. Attempt to turn Jesus' responses into boundary statements:

a. How did His responses define who He was?

b. How did they demonstrate who God was to Him?

c. How did they demonstrate His way of doing ministry?

▼ ▼ ▼ ▼ ▼ ▼ ▼ ▼ ▼ ▼ ▼ ▼ ▼ ▼ ▼ ▼ ▼ ▼
Applying the Text   15 minutes

There are two sides to boundary building. One is respecting others' boundaries even if they don't (e.g., knowing when not to give advice). The second is deciding how to help others respect our boundaries, even if they don't want to (e.g., knowing how to build healthy space into need-based relationships).

10. Look at the three categories of boundaries in our text:

    ❏ Physical: Includes time, space, privacy, sexuality
    ❏ Personal: Includes friendship, choices, emotions, family
    ❏ Spiritual: Includes faith, risk, accountability, authority

    a. How can leaders respect others' boundaries in these areas?

b. How can leaders develop and maintain their own boundaries in these areas?

11. People with boundaries learn to deal with difficult situations in a positive manner. In what sorts of situations might you want to use each of the following phrases?

☐ "We need to discuss a better time to talk."
☐ "No, I can't do that at this time. I'll let you know when."
☐ "That makes me uncomfortable—could you give me some space?"
☐ "I understand that you feel I let you down, but I had not indicated accountability to you in this area."
☐ "I need to go."
☐ "I have promised my husband or wife that I won't be alone in these situations with a member of the opposite sex."
☐ "I don't take calls at supper or past 9:00 at night."

12. Recall the two situations in the role play (question 3).

a. What boundaries were broken?

b. What would have been some positive boundary-building statements?

13. Which of the following "boundary difficulties" apply to you?

☐ I get too entwined in people's lives when trying to help them.
☐ I allow people to use me because I get too close to their situations.
☐ When things don't go well with individuals or the group I lead, I get stressed out very easily.
☐ I respond to every criticism that people have of me and the group I lead.
☐ I can be pushy with people who aren't listening to me.
☐ I put way too much time into preparing for my group.

▼ ▼ ▼ ▼ ▼ ▼ ▼ ▼ ▼ ▼ ▼ ▼ ▼ ▼ ▼ ▼ ▼ ▼ ▼
Assignment   10 minutes

Decide which of the following homework electives you will do. Make sure that your choices are reasonable and will be performed by everyone prior to the next meeting.

Elective 1: Reflection—Continue the journal you began after session 1. To guide your exploration, go back to questions 10 and 13, and mark down all of the areas you struggle with. Then ask yourself these questions for each one you marked:

▶ Why do I struggle with this particular area?
▶ How can I build boundaries to protect this area?
▶ What are positive statements I can craft to help me articulate this boundary?

Elective 2: Project—Building boundaries is a significant human activity. Your assignment is to locate no fewer than ten ways that society builds boundaries (for example: we have markers to show where one property ends and another begins).

▶ What do these boundaries teach about basic human need?
▶ Why do you think Christians have difficulty building personal, physical, and spiritual boundaries?

Prayer   10 minutes

Adapt these prayer ground rules to your situation.

▶ Be conversational. The group is not a place for impressive theological prayers. Keep prayer relaxed and relational.

▶ Be brief. The first people who pray in a group setting are usually comfortable praying in public. They can end up covering all requests in lengthy prayers. A good practice is to hold the first two "pray-ers" to two sentences each.

▶ Be courteous. Keep requests personal or limited to intimate family and friends. Be as brief as possible when sharing requests so that others have time to share.

▶ Be sensitive. A small group is not the place to attempt to counsel ("fix") another person.

▶ Be real. Most of the prayer times in this resource encourage you to respond to the issue being studied. Since the group committed to confidentiality in session one, you can be honest about what God needs to do in your life.

Stand in a circle. Allow each person to respond to the statement, "Today I learned that I need to. . . ." Hold hands if you are comfortable doing so. Let each person pray aloud, beginning with the leader. Consider praying by name for the leaders in your group, asking God to help each of you build healthy boundaries and respect others' boundaries. If you would rather pray silently, please say "Amen" aloud to let the other people know you are finished.

Reference Notes

Setting: This event took place at the beginning of Christ's ministry. Several significant themes underlay this event. First, the "second

Adam" (Christ) had to face temptation as the first Adam did, but Christ was able to stand firm. Second, most great men and women of the Bible had significant desert experiences: Moses, John the Baptist, David, Jeremiah, Paul, the disciples, and Hagar, to name a few. The desert experience allowed each person the opportunity to die to parts of their lives and to express complete obedience to God.

Next: The events of Jesus' time in the desert followed on the heels of His baptism, and "next" implies a seamless thought linking the events together. Jesus was validated by the Spirit at His baptism and sent by the Spirit to the desert for testing so that He could minister by the Spirit in the world.

the Test: Although Satan was the form of the temptation, God allowed the Test to strengthen Jesus' character and faith. God does not author sin nor encourage us to do so, but He will allow us to face circumstances that stretch our faith and drive us to reliance on Him.

Since you are God's Son: Some scholars have understood Satan's first words as a taunt, questioning whether Jesus was really the Son of God: "If you are. . . ." But Eugene Peterson has, I believe, picked up on the spirit of Satan's agenda: not to question Jesus' sonship, but to "reflect" with Him on its meaning. In Genesis Satan did not question Adam and Eve's position in the garden; he sought to reflect with them on how to expand it. So in this first temptation, Satan tried to get Jesus "thinking."

It takes more than bread to stay alive: Jesus replied to the first temptation without flinching. Recognizing that Satan was trying to get Him to act apart from God (albeit in a manner that Jesus could easily have accomplished, as we see in the feeding of the four and five thousand), Jesus quoted Deuteronomy 8:3. The spirit of Deuteronomy 8:3 is total, absolute, unflinching dependence on God. By His response, Jesus was signaling His willingness to totally obey and submit to God.

Don't you dare test the Lord your God: Jesus' response is from Deuteronomy 6:16. Appropriating special protection from God was wrong. Instead, He was to trust God's provision and timing.

Worship the Lord your God: Even at the beginning of His ministry, Jesus knew He had to suffer. Instead of turning away from the cross, however, He set His mind and heart like flint and worshiped God, even when that worship was costly.

Angels came: The end of the passage marks fulfillment of everything that Satan was promising Christ. First, He was fed. Then, the angels cared for Him. And third, He began His ministry.

▼ ▼ ▼ ▼ ▼ ▼ ▼ ▼ ▼ ▼ ▼ ▼ ▼ ▼ ▼ ▼ ▼ ▼
Food for Thought

Here are eight boundary myths that sound like truth but aren't:

- ▶ Myth #1: If I set boundaries, I'm being selfish.
- ▶ Myth #2: Boundaries are a sign of disobedience.
- ▶ Myth #3: If I begin setting boundaries, I will be hurt by others.
- ▶ Myth #4: If I set boundaries, I will hurt others.
- ▶ Myth #5: Boundaries mean that I am angry.
- ▶ Myth #6: When others set boundaries, it injures me.
- ▶ Myth #7: Boundaries cause feelings of guilt.
- ▶ Myth #8: Boundaries are permanent, and I'm afraid of burning my bridges.

Dr. Henry Cloud and Dr. John Townsend,
*Boundaries: When to Say YES, When to Say NO,
To Take Control of Your Life,*
(Grand Rapids, Mich.: Zondervan,1992),
pp. 83-103.

Proactive Covenant Making

▼ ▼ ▼ ▼ ▼ ▼ ▼ ▼ ▼ ▼ ▼ ▼ ▼ ▼ ▼ ▼ ▼ ▼ ▼ ▼
Overview   5 minutes

❶ *Allow several group members to share what they
learned from their homework (if the group did not do homework, encourage members to recap what they learned from the
last session).*
*Then ask someone to read aloud this story and the objec-
tives that follow.*

I will never forget the last evening of my first mission service
project. I had taken a group to spend a week with an organization that worked among poverty-stricken folks living in the
mountains. On our first day of the project we had received
extensive training in team-building and empowerment techniques. We made agreements to listen, be a team, and include
everyone in decisions and work.

It had been a great week for me. My team had designed and
constructed a goat barn using crude materials. The outdoor
work and physical challenge was exhilarating.

That last night we sat around the campfire and processed
how the week's events had affected us. To help us share, we
made symbolic gifts for each other.

My gift from my team was a block of wood (don't draw too
many conclusions yet!) with one large spike in the middle and
five much smaller ones on the outside. When I asked about the
meaning of the gift, they shared very sensitively that I was the

one who had made the project run, and they had been my helpers.

Perhaps remembering our empowerment training, I became uncomfortable. "You mean I did all of the work and you stood around?" I expected to hear, "Of course not!"

"Yes," they said, "that is what we mean."

I was hurt. How could they say that? I had allowed them to do some of the big jobs. And after all, I was the only one with building experience!

Of course, looking back I now realize how overpowering I could (and can) be. I believe their honesty in that setting forced me to listen, respond, and apologize.

It was the agreement (covenant) we made at the beginning of the week that made the fireside confrontation possible. The agreement raised their expectations. They had a standard by which to judge my leadership, something they had never possessed before. No longer could I fly around and dispense orders and advice. They wanted input and the opportunity to grow.

A covenant like this helps to guide relationships and promote growth. In this session we will:

> ▶ learn why covenants are important
> ▶ examine how God covenants with us
> ▶ develop ground rules in response to real problems
> ▶ determine how ground rules might help us respond to difficult situations in our lives

▼ ▼ ▼ ▼ ▼ ▼ ▼ ▼ ▼ ▼ ▼ ▼ ▼ ▼ ▼ ▼ ▼ ▼
Beginning   20 minutes

❶ *Go around the room and allow each person to answer the first question before moving to the next one. The leader should answer #1 first, but after that, let someone else go first.*

1. Think back to a small group you were in that was unhealthy. Look over the list below and see which of these characteristics (and other characteristics you can think of) were present in that group:

   ❏ group members came late
   ❏ the meeting consistently ran overtime

❏ almost nobody came prepared
❏ one or two strong personalities dominated
❏ the leader rambled, or was boring, or_____(you fill in the blank)
❏ unspoken tensions grew until the group could not function anymore
❏ other:

2. What are three group characteristics that are important to you, that you look for in a healthy group, and why?

3. What one or two negative group characteristics irritate you so much that you would be tempted to leave the group?

▼ ▼
Worship   10 minutes—Optional

▶ Psalm 115 is based on God's faithfulness. Read it responsively.

▶ Then, sing several praise songs/hymns that reflect the faithfulness of God ("Great is Thy Faithfulness," "The Steadfast Love of the Lord"). If you are uncomfortable singing, perhaps several individuals can either read or recite a praise song or hymn, or the group can reflect together on the meaning of God's faithfulness.

▶ After singing or sharing, allow time to give God praise and thanksgiving for His faithfulness, perhaps with prayer and/or a testimony time.

▼ ▼
The Text   5 minutes

Covenants allow Christians to define who they are and how they
will live together in community. When Christians think of a
covenant, they often think of Exodus 20 (the Ten Commandments),
Genesis 1 and 2 (God's covenants with Adam and Eve), Genesis 12
(God's call to Abram and Sarah), and the various Lord's Supper
(God's "new covenant") passages. But Deuteronomy, whose
name literally means "Second (Giving of the) Law," is a complete
book on covenanting. It contains a series of sermons Moses gave
just before the Israelites entered the Promised Land. The
covenant spelled out what was expected of Israel and what was
promised by God, including rewards and punishments for obedience or disobedience. Deuteronomy 7 is in a section dealing with
the worship of other gods.

❶ *Have someone read the text aloud. You may also read
some or all of the reference notes on pages 46-47.*

The LORD did not set his affection on you and choose you
because you were more numerous than other peoples, for you
were the fewest of all peoples. But **it was because the LORD
loved you** and kept **the oath he swore to your forefathers** that
he brought you out with a mighty hand and redeemed you from
the land of slavery. . . . Know therefore that the LORD your God
is God; **he is the faithful God**, keeping his covenant of love to a
thousand generations of those who love him and keep his commands. But those who hate him he will repay to their face by
destruction; he will not be slow to repay to their face those who
hate him. Therefore, take care to follow the commands, decrees
and laws I give you today.
  If you pay attention to these laws and are careful to follow
them, then **the LORD your God will keep his covenant of love**
with you, as he swore to your forefathers. He will love you and
bless you and increase your numbers. He will bless the fruit of
your womb, the crops of your land—your grain, new wine and
oil—the calves of your herds and the lambs of your flocks in the
land that he swore to your forefathers to give you. You will be
blessed more than any other people. . . .

(Deuteronomy 7:7-14)

40

4. God did not choose to operate in relationship with Israel because these people had endearing qualities. What two reasons does Moses give for God's relationship with Israel?

5. This passage provides a glimpse into certain characteristics of Israel (what they brought to the negotiating table). Circle everything that offers information about Israel. How would you summarize what this passage informs us about Israel?

6. This passage provides a glimpse into certain characteristics of God. Underline everything that offers information about God. How would you summarize what this passage teaches about God?

7. This covenant spelled out expectations for Israel. The expectations included how the people were to think about

God and how they were to relate to God. Locate the expectations. What was expected of Israel?

8. This covenant also spelled out expectations for God. The expectations included how He was to respond either to obedience or disobedience. Locate the expectations. What was expected of God?

▼ ▼ ▼ ▼ ▼ ▼ ▼ ▼ ▼ ▼ ▼ ▼ ▼ ▼ ▼ ▼ ▼
Applying the Text   20 minutes

In the business and social world, few people still operate on a handshake basis. In order to transact business, they rely on covenants, usually called contracts. Contracts are created in order to protect all parties of an agreement from the many ways in which human sin can negate promises that have been made. Within a company, business leaders create mission and vision statements, set sales goals and budgets, and define policies—all in order to clarify who the company is, what it does, how employees relate, and where the company hopes to be in one, two, or five years.

In the Christian world, covenants serve similar purposes. They allow us to define: who we are (group identity), what we do (group function), how we relate (group communication), and where we are going (group goals). Explicit covenants are useful for discipleship groups, task groups (such as committees or Elder Boards), classes—any group of people that needs to agree on its identity, goals, activities, and ground rules. A typical covenant for a home-based small group may be found on pages 47-48.

Some people find the term *covenant* intimidating because of its heavy biblical connotations. You may prefer to speak simply of goals or ground rules. Some groups like the idea of signing a covenant, while others choose to discuss ground rules and agree on them verbally.

9. Why might simple written covenants be helpful in the following situations?

   a. two Christians who meet for breakfast to talk and pray together

   b. a group of Christians meeting over the course of months to plan a mission conference or retreat

   c. a new staff member is hired—she is a layperson hired from within the church membership

   d. a Sunday school class

10. Write a covenant for one of the situations in question 9, following this outline:

    Who we are (group identity):

    What we do (group function):

    How we relate (group communication):

11. What might be three first-year goals for the group you just described?

12. Turn each of the following negative group characteristics into a group covenant statement.

   ❐ group members gossip
   ❐ group members put each other down
   ❐ group members come late
   ❐ there is tension about what the group should be doing
   ❐ the meetings meander with no purpose
   ❐ some sensitive group items have leaked into the church
   ❐ group members exhibit little commitment to work or participate
   ❐ some group members are ignored

13. Turn to the group covenant on pages 47-48.

   a. What do you like about it?

   b. What would you add or change?

14. (Optional—if your leader group is ongoing) Complete or adapt the group covenant on page 47 and have each member sign or verbally affirm it.

▼ ▼ ▼ ▼ ▼ ▼ ▼ ▼ ▼ ▼ ▼ ▼ ▼ ▼ ▼ ▼ ▼ ▼
Assignment   10 minutes

Decide which of the following homework electives you will do. Make sure that your choices are reasonable and will be performed by everyone prior to the next meeting.

Elective 1: Reflection—Covenants create disciplines, which in turn create order and life stability. Many "good" people wonder why their lives feel out of control and disorderly. Perhaps they need to learn how to covenant with themselves and those they relate to. To reflectively ponder the importance of covenanting, choose one relationship (preferably a close one) in your life and complete the following:

- ▶ list everything good about the relationship
- ▶ list everything about the relationship that is bad or needs work
- ▶ group both good and bad parts of the relationship under the four headings of covenant: who we are; what we do; how we relate; where we are going
- ▶ create positive covenant statements to turn the negatives into positives
- ▶ prayerfully consider discussing what you have learned with the other person

Elective 2: Project—How covenants work.

- ▶ Sometime before the next meeting, find a contract (from a home sale, your job, a friend's job, a car purchase, etc.).
- ▶ Read the contract carefully. As you read, write down the sins that the contract attempts to rectify (for instance, a home purchase and sale agreement lists a date for closing on the home because some people procrastinate).
- ▶ How does the contract promote positive interactions?

▼ ▼ ▼ ▼ ▼ ▼ ▼ ▼ ▼ ▼ ▼ ▼ ▼ ▼ ▼ ▼ ▼ ▼
Prayer 5 minutes

Stand in a circle. Allow each person to complete the sentence, "One thing (fear, apathy, past hurt) in my life that keeps me from deeper relationships is. . . ." Hold hands if you are comfortable doing so. Let each person pray aloud, beginning with the leader. Pray for each other by name based on the statements that have been made. If you would rather pray silently, please say "Amen" aloud to let the other people know you are finished.

▼ ▼ ▼ ▼ ▼ ▼ ▼ ▼ ▼ ▼ ▼ ▼ ▼ ▼ ▼ ▼ ▼ ▼ ▼
Reference Notes

Setting: Moses and the Israelites were poised at the brink of the Promised Land, which God had promised their ancestors for many years. As part of their preparation for entry, Moses delivered a series of sermons that form the structure of Deuteronomy. Deuteronomy is not just a series of sermons, but the text of a covenant made between God and Israel. Deuteronomy 7 is part of Moses' second sermon. The chapter provides both a historic glimpse of the land the people will inhabit (verses 1-6) and a future look (verses 7-26) at the temptations and possibilities in the land.

it was because the LORD loved you: By this time Israel had grown from one man (Abraham) into a large nation. The people were about to cross into the Promised Land, where God had already assured victory. Individuals and nations in such a position can easily be deceived into thinking their good fortune is related to something they do or who they are. Because Israel was set apart by God, she would face this temptation throughout her history. So God wanted to make it clear that it was not anything Israel possessed, nor who the people were, that dictated His relationship with them. It was solely His love, His choice, His promises, His affection. The intent of these words was to humble the Israelites and to give them a healthy perspective as they embarked on a new era in their history.

the oath he swore to your forefathers: God made promises to Abraham, Isaac, and Jacob throughout the events recorded in the book of Genesis.

he is the faithful God: In the covenant He was making with His people, God indicated His intent to keep every promise He had made. Because of His dealings with Israel from the time of Abraham, God could appeal to the past (in essence, "I have been faithful") as a down payment on the future (in essence, "I will continue to be faithful").

the Lord your God will keep his covenant of love: The only significant time in which Israel enjoyed the blessings of verses 13-14 was when King David and then King Solomon ruled them.

Sample Group Covenant

1. The reason our group exists is:

2. Our specific group goals include:

3. We meet ____ time(s) a month, and this covenant will be in effect for ____ weeks/months. At the end of the covenant period, we will evaluate our progress and growth.

4. We will meet on _____ (day of week), from ____ until ____ (beginning and ending times).

5. Our meetings will be held at _____ (place[s]).

6. We will use _____ as a basis for study or training.

7. We will agree on one or more of the following disciplines:

   ► Acceptance: We will affirm one another's contributions.
   ► Confidentiality: What is spoken in the group remains in the group.
   ► Openness: As we are able, we will be honest and forthright with one another.
   ► Graciousness: We will not speak about a person when he or she is not present.
   ► Self-discipline: When the group agrees to homework, we will come prepared.
   ► Courtesy: When the group meets, we will come on time.
   ► Listening: None of us will monopolize our time together, making it difficult for others to speak.

8. Other possible ground rules:
- ► Food (who's responsible for bringing what)
- ► Child care
- ► Group leadership (one leader with an apprentice, or rotating leadership)
- ► Growth or Multiplication (if a priority, discuss plan)

Signed: _____

Managing Resources

▼ ▼ ▼ ▼ ▼ ▼ ▼ ▼ ▼ ▼ ▼ ▼ ▼ ▼ ▼ ▼ ▼ ▼

Overview   10 minutes

❶ *Allow several group members to share what they learned from their homework. If the group did not do homework, encourage members to recap what they learned from the last session. Then ask someone to read the following material aloud.*

"I am leading a group that has become apathetic and lethargic. What can I do?"

"My group members come so late that we don't have enough time to do our work!"

"We have one person who monopolizes discussion. What should we do about it?"

Lay leaders all over the country ask questions like these. As I coach leaders, I have developed a simple response: Write a covenant, and enforce it!

In our last session we discussed the importance of forming a covenant. We learned that covenants help a group or ministry define who they are, what they do, how they relate, and where they're going. We intentionally left out an important part of covenants—the mandate they give leaders to hold groups and ministries to disciplines, direction, and the implementation of resources. That mandate is the basis for group management, or what Christians often call "stewardship." Effective leaders

49

understand how to arrive at the mandate (covenant making) and how to enforce it (management).

A steward manages somebody else's property. Christians understand that we are stewards of everything God has given us—it belongs to Him, and we are expected to manage it for the benefit of God's kingdom and for God's glory. In the case of a group or ministry, the group belongs first to God and second to the group, and the leader is responsible for managing or stewarding the group's resources on behalf of God and the group. All group members are accountable to God for being good stewards of the group's resources, but the buck stops with the leader. If everyone in the group has agreed to the ground rules or covenant, then the group has said, "These are your standards for managing our resources."

In this session we will:

► learn about biblical management
► discuss the areas of group life we need to manage: time, resources, and gifts
► share areas that we want to manage better

▼ ▼ ▼ ▼ ▼ ▼ ▼ ▼ ▼ ▼ ▼ ▼ ▼ ▼ ▼ ▼ ▼ ▼ ▼
Beginning   15 minutes

❶ *In preparation for this activity, write the brief statements under question 1 on separate slips of paper. Fold the papers and place them in a hat. There should be no more than ten slips of paper. Go around the room and allow each person to draw and respond to his or her slip of paper. When one person has drawn and responded to what is written on his or her slip of paper, have that person return the slip and shake up the hat before the next person draws. Go around the room twice. If a person draws the same slip as he or she did last time, let him or her re-draw.*

1. Allow each person to respond to at least two of the following statements, drawn at random from a bowl or other container:

   ❑ If I won a million dollars I would. . . .
   ❑ If I had one month and the resources to do whatever I wanted, I would. . . .

❐ If each day had thirty hours, with the six extra hours I would. . . .
❐ If I could have giftedness (expertise, ability) in any one area, I would like. . . .
❐ If I could travel anywhere in the world to see one special place, I would go to. . . .
❐ If each day had twenty hours (four fewer than now), to make up the lost time I would cut. . . .
❐ If I won a thousand dollars I would. . . .
❐ If I lost everything I own in one day, I would. . . .
❐ If a large vein of gold were discovered on property I own, I would. . . .
❐ If I paid dearly for land in Florida only to discover it was swamp land, I would. . . .

2. When it comes to management of my time, resources, and gifts, I am:

❐ completely focused and disciplined
❐ completely unfocused and undisciplined
❐ sometimes focused and disciplined, but mostly not
❐ generally focused and disciplined

▼ ▼ ▼ ▼ ▼ ▼ ▼ ▼ ▼ ▼ ▼ ▼ ▼ ▼ ▼ ▼
Worship   10 minutes—Optional

To phrase Christian stewardship in the language of worship, we worship, praise, and serve God, the Creator and Sustainer of all that is.

▶ Read Psalm 148. Read it responsively, with half the group reading a verse and then the other half reading the next verse. Or, have one or several people read it.

▶ As the psalm is read, listen for objects and living beings that God created. After the psalm is read, discuss the beauty, creativity, and power evident in these created things.

▶ Close by singing a praise song or two to God (for example, "Be Exalted").

▼ ▼ ▼ ▼ ▼ ▼ ▼ ▼ ▼ ▼ ▼ ▼ ▼ ▼ ▼ ▼ ▼ ▼ ▼

The Text 5 minutes

Management shows up often in Jesus' teachings. For those who believe time, money, and other resources are not spiritual subjects, Jesus responds with such statements as, "Where your treasure is, there your heart will be also" (Matthew 6:21). In the following passage, Jesus connects management to our relationship with Him, the "Master." He asserts that a constant state of readiness will keep us focused on managing our assets for His purposes, not ours.

❶ *Have someone read the text aloud. You may also read some or all of the reference notes on pages 58-59.*

"Keep your shirts on; keep the lights on! Be like house servants waiting for their master to come back from his honeymoon, awake and ready to open the door when he arrives and knocks. Lucky the servants whom the master finds on watch! **He'll put on an apron**, sit them at the table, and serve them a meal, sharing his wedding feast with them. It doesn't matter what time of the night he arrives; they're awake—and so blessed!

"You know that **if the house owner had known** what night the burglar was coming, he wouldn't have stayed out late and left the place unlocked. So don't you be slovenly and careless. Just when you don't expect him, the Son of Man will show up."

Peter said, "Master, **are you telling this story just for us? Or is it for everybody?**"

The Master said, "Let me ask you: Who is the dependable manager, full of common sense, that the master puts in charge of his staff to feed them well and on time? He is a blessed man if when the master shows up he's doing his job. But if he says to himself, 'The master is certainly taking his time,' begins maltreating the servants and maids, throws parties for his friends, and gets drunk, the master will walk in when he least expects it, give him the thrashing of his life, and put him back in the kitchen peeling potatoes.

"The servant who knows what his master wants and ignores it, or insolently does whatever he pleases, **will be thoroughly thrashed**. But if he does a poor job through ignorance, he'll get off with a slap on the hand. Great gifts mean great responsibilities; greater gifts, greater responsibilities!"

(Luke 12:35-48, MSG)

Understanding the Text ▼▼▼▼▼▼▼▼▼▼▼▼▼▼▼▼▼▼▼ 15 minutes

3. In Christ's day, slaves had no rights. Therefore, it was logical to presume that they would wait in fear for their master's return. Why might Jesus have employed the example of slaves in relation to stewardship?

4. Imagine how slaves must think and act when they are not sure of their master's return. What does a slave's mindset have to do with stewardship?

5. In the second paragraph, Jesus used the image of a homeowner and a thief. An unprepared homeowner is called slovenly and careless. What does it mean to be slovenly and careless?

6. Jesus talks about two managers: one with common sense, and one who abuses his position. Contrast the two. Attempt to summarize their differences in one character quality. What is it?

7. The passage closes with the statement: "Great gifts mean great responsibilities; greater gifts, greater responsibilities!" How is a Christian leader to interpret such a statement?

8. How do you respond to the images employed in this passage?
   ❏ I'm ready to do what it takes to be a steward.
   ❏ I'd like to be ready, but I'm scared of the responsibility.
   ❏ I'd rather not have to take on such responsibility.
   ❏ I don't want to be in charge of anything.

▼ ▼ ▼ ▼ ▼ ▼ ▼ ▼ ▼ ▼ ▼ ▼ ▼ ▼ ▼ ▼ ▼
Applying the Text   20 minutes

9. In the introduction to this chapter a "leader's mandate" was mentioned. Such a mandate is usually located in a group covenant. To illustrate, locate issues in the following group covenant that direct the leader in his/her application of leadership.

Group Covenant:
1. Our group exists to follow Christ in community and to make Christ known in our circles of influence.
2. Our objectives are to: grow in our faith; learn to pray; study God's Word; support each other through our various ups and downs; and participate in two one-day service projects by the end of the year.
3. We meet three times per month; this covenant begins in September and ends in December.
4. We meet on Tuesdays from 7:00 - 9:00 P.M. at Steve's home.
5. We are open to new members, although at times we may close in the middle of a study.
6. We agree to: not discuss another member unless he/she is present; attend and do all work that is agreed upon; hold what we hear as a group in confidence.
7. Fred will lead our worship; Samantha will be our hostess; Susan will lead our times of prayer; Jeff will be our apprentice leader; Karen will be our leader.
8. Our schedule is: 7:00-7:10 refreshments; 7:10-7:25 fellowship/community building; 7:25-8:00 study time; 8:00-8:25 sharing, prayer, and group business.

10. Based on the covenant above, how would you expect the leader to respond to several group members who do not want to accept the friend of a member as a newcomer?

11. How would you expect the above leader to respond to the group when several members want to study a third straight book by a popular Christian author?

12. What are three specific goals this group could set for itself during its first year?

13. Leaders help a group manage its time properly.

    a. What are some ways in which time can be abused by a group?

    b. What suggestions would you give a leader to keep a group focused according to its covenant?

14. Leaders help a group manage its resources (energy, meeting place, activities, ideas, studies, etc.) properly.

    a. What are some ways in which groups can mismanage their resources?

    b. What suggestions would you give a leader to effectively use the group's resources?

15. Leaders help a group manage its gifts (spiritual gifts) properly.

    a. In what ways can groups ignore people's gifts?

    b. What suggestions would you give to a leader to become aware of the contributions group members can make?

Assignment ▼▼▼▼ ▼▼▼▼▼▼▼▼▼▼▼▼▼ 10 minutes

Decide which of the following homework electives you will do. Make sure that your choices are reasonable and will be performed by everyone prior to the next meeting.

Elective 1: Reflection—How a leader manages resources is clear to objective observers and a good indication of leadership effectiveness. Your reflections on management are therefore important. Reflect on your strengths and weaknesses in management of your personal . . .

▶ time
▶ resources (including money, home, etc.)
▶ gifts and abilities

Reflect on your leadership strengths and weaknesses. How do you manage group . . .

▶ time
▶ resources
▶ gifts

Elective 2: Project—Take a close look at two items that are effective barometers of stewardship: your calendar or planning book (or lack thereof); and your checkbook. Answer these questions for each:

▶ What priorities do they show? What is important to me and my family?
▶ What clues can I find by examining how they are used and how they are maintained?
▶ Based on my scrutiny of them, what is one thing that I need to change?

▼▼▼ ▼▼▼▼▼▼▼▼ ▼ ▼▼▼▼ ▼▼ ▼▼
Prayer   5 minutes

Stand in a circle. Allow each person to ask briefly for one prayer request. Hold hands if you are comfortable doing so. Let each person pray aloud, beginning with the leader. Pray for each other by name. If you would rather pray silently, please say "Amen" aloud to let the other people know you are finished.

▼ ▼▼▼▼ ▼▼▼▼▼▼ ▼ ▼▼▼ ▼▼▼ ▼
Reference Notes

Setting: Luke 12 contains a series of sermons and events loosely tied to the theme of being watchful. Jesus begins Luke 12 by warning His disciples not to be like the Pharisees. He then tells the story of the rich fool who died even while planning to build bigger barns. Luke 12:22-34 contains teaching about worry, with promises for God's provisions as we learn to focus on God's kingdom. Verses 35-48 then continue the theme of being watchful and focused on God's agenda, not ours.

Keep your shirts on; keep the lights on!: Another way to say it is, "gird up your loins." Eastern men wore long tunics that, when the men were in a state of activity or readiness, needed to be tucked in.

He'll put on an apron: Typical of the unpredictable Christ, He "turns the tables." Instead of the servant feeding the master, the master will feed the servant who is ready. A powerful change of direction for listeners who expected the servant to sit the master down and feed him.

if the house owner had known: This phrase is spoken in such a way that we must presume that there was a recent burglary well known to Christ and the audience. Jesus therefore resorted to a current event to illustrate His point about readiness.

are you telling this story just for us? We can assume that this passage connects to the previous passage (Luke 12:22-34), which begins, "Jesus said to his disciples . . ." Peter, typical spokesperson for the disciples, questioned whether the teaching was for all believers or for the church leaders. As we shall see in evaluating the next phrase, it was for leaders.

will be thoroughly thrashed: Several points can be made about this phrase. First, Jesus' using slavery as an illustration is not either a support or condemnation of slavery. Second, at first glance this statement seems insensitive—because slaves do indeed get beaten. But this is an analogy—those who are put in leadership positions are expected to lead well. Jesus says elsewhere that "anyone who breaks one of the least of these commandments and teaches others to do the same will be called least in the kingdom of heaven" (Matthew 5:19).

▼ ▼ ▼ ▼ ▼ ▼ ▼ ▼ ▼ ▼ ▼ ▼ ▼ ▼ ▼ ▼ ▼ ▼ ▼ ▼
Additional Resources:

1. MacDonald, Gordon. *Ordering Your Private World.* Nashville, Tenn.: Nelson, 1985.

2. Minirth, Frank, et al. *The Workaholic and His Family.* Grand Rapids, Mich.: Baker, 1985.

3. White, John. *Excellence in Leadership.* Downers Grove, Ill.: InterVarsity, 1986.

Persistent Prayer

Overview   10 minutes

❶ *Allow several group members to share what they
learned from their homework (if the group did not do homework, encourage members to recap what they learned from the
last session).*

*Then ask someone to read aloud this story and the objec-
tives that follow.*

I am the kind of person who does nothing halfheartedly. I want
to master everything. I am a person of action and energy. As a
result, prayer has always been a source of discomfort for me. No
matter how I try, I cannot feel that I master it. If anything, it
masters me.

I have tried everything, from prayer lists to days spent in
prayer and fasting. And even though I have been greatly blessed
many times, I have never felt comfortable on a long-term basis
with prayer.

I now know that is the way it is supposed to be. In *Prayer:
Finding the Heart's True Home*, Richard Foster helped to make
me aware that prayer is a dynamic interaction with God that
cannot be solved by formulas or lists. This quote from Foster
sums up much of what I have learned:

> We today yearn for prayer and hide from prayer. We are
> attracted to it and repelled by it. We believe prayer is

something we should do, even something we want to do, but it seems like a chasm stands between us and actually praying. We experience the agony of prayerlessness.

We are not quite sure what holds us back. Of course we are busy with work and family obligations, but that is only a smoke screen. Our busyness seldom keeps us from eating or sleeping or making love. No, there is something deeper, more profound keeping us in check. In reality, there are a number of "somethings" preventing us, all of which we will explore in due time. But for now there is one "something" that needs immediate attention. It is the notion—almost universal among us modern high achievers—that we have to have everything "just right" in order to pray. . . . Our problem is that we assume prayer is something to master the way we master algebra or auto mechanics. That puts us in the "on-top" position, where we are competent and in control. But when praying, we come "underneath," where we calmly and deliberately surrender control and become incompetent. (Richard Foster, *Prayer: Finding the Heart's True Home*, HarperSanFrancisco, pp. 7-8)

In this session we will:

- ▶ share our feelings, strengths, and weaknesses in relation to prayer
- ▶ learn various facets of prayer
- ▶ practice praying together in a guided experience of prayer

▼▼▼▼▼▼▼▼▼▼▼▼▼▼▼▼▼▼
Beginning   15 minutes

❶ *Go around the room and allow each person to answer the first question before moving on to the next one. The leader should answer first each time.*

1. Tell an answer you received to a prayer that you (or another) had prayed.

2. Of the following, check those you feel comfortable doing, and circle those you are not as comfortable with.

❏ worshiping spontaneously
❏ worshiping according to a formal written plan
❏ confessing your sin individually before God
❏ confessing sin publicly (in a group or one-on-one setting)
❏ thanking God publicly for His blessings
❏ praying in private for others
❏ praying publicly for others
❏ praying with a person for his or her healing

▼ ▼ ▼ ▼ ▼ ▼ ▼ ▼ ▼ ▼ ▼ ▼ ▼ ▼ ▼ ▼ ▼ ▼ ▼
The Text   5 minutes

In response to a question asked by His disciples, Jesus provides a brief overview of significant issues related to prayer.

❶ *Have someone read the text aloud. You may also read some or all of the reference notes on page 69.*

One day Jesus was praying in a certain place. When he finished, one of his disciples said to him, "Lord, teach us to pray, just as John taught his disciples."

He said to them, "When you pray, say: "'Father, hallowed be your name, your kingdom come. Give us each day our daily bread. Forgive us our sins, for we also forgive everyone who sins against us. **And lead us not into temptation.**'"

Then he said to them, "Suppose one of you has a friend, and he goes to him at midnight and says, 'Friend, lend me three loaves of bread, because a friend of mine on a journey has come to me, and I have nothing to set before him.'

"Then the one inside answers, 'Don't bother me. The door is already locked, and my children are with me in bed. I can't get up and give you anything.' I tell you, though he will not get up and give him the bread because he is his friend, yet because of **the man's persistence** he will get up and give him as much as he needs.

"So I say to you: Ask and it will be given to you; seek and you will find; knock and the door will be opened to you. For everyone who asks receives; he who seeks finds; and to him who knocks, the door will be opened.

"Which of you fathers, if your son asks for a fish, will give him a snake instead? Or if he asks for an egg, will give him a scorpion? If you then, though you are evil, know how to give good gifts to your children, how much more will your Father in heaven give **the Holy Spirit** to those who ask him!"

(Luke 11:1-13)

▼ ▼ ▼ ▼ ▼ ▼ ▼ ▼ ▼ ▼ ▼ ▼ ▼ ▼ ▼ ▼ ▼
Understanding the Text   20 minutes

3. Luke 11:1 provides the setting for this teaching: The disciples had located Jesus praying on His own, something He did on many occasions.

    a. Why do you think Jesus had not formally taught His disciples about prayer?

    b. What might observing Jesus' private prayer life have taught the disciples?

4. There are five requests in Luke's version of the Lord's Prayer. The first two address our relationship with God.

    ❏ hallowed be your name
    ❏ your kingdom come

    a. What do you think we are asking for or affirming in each of these first two statements?

b. How are these different from what we normally think of as prayer requests?

c. Our prayers most often ask God to do something. By contrast, what do these prayers ask of us?

5. These next three requests deal with our individual and interpersonal needs.
   ❐ give us each day our daily bread
   ❐ forgive us our sins, for we also forgive everyone who sins against us
   ❐ lead us not into temptation

   a. What is being asked for in each of these requests?

   b. What life priorities do these requests reflect?

6. What does the parable of verses 5-8 teach us about how to pray?

7. What does it mean to ask, seek, and knock?

8. Think of some examples of asking, seeking, and knocking in your own prayer life, or that of someone you know.

9. From verses 11-13 we can presume that God acts kindly on our behalf, as if He were a good father.

    a. What does it mean that He will "give the Holy Spirit to those who ask him?"

    b. How is the Spirit an extension of the Father's kindness?

Applying the Text   15 minutes

10. The Lord's Prayer offers us a prayer model that, when used flexibly, guides our interaction with God. For each of the following aspects of prayer, list what for you personally are hindrances that keep you from effectively praying in this manner and aids that might encourage you to pray in this manner.

    a. worship (hallowed be your name)—we lift up God's name

       ❏ hindrances

       ❏ aids

b. intercession (your kingdom come)—we pray for God's reign and will in every arena, from our hearts to our friends to our world

❑ hindrances

❑ aids

c. petition (give us each day our daily bread)—we pray for our needs

❑ hindrances

❑ aids

d. confession (forgive us our sins as we forgive those who sin against us)—we confess our sins and forgive others

❑ hindrances

❑ aids

e. supplication (lead us not into temptation)—we pray for protection from evil

❑ hindrances

❑ aids

11. Respond (on the following page) to this statement:
Leaders should attempt to bring the names of those they work with on a daily basis before God in prayer.

a. How does this statement make you feel?

b. What benefits may come from praying for those you work with?

c. What time of day is best for you to pray for those you lead or work with?

d. How might this group help you be accountable?

Prayer and Worship   15 minutes

Experience prayer together. For the next twenty minutes, stop talking about prayer and "do it!" You will spend four minutes in each of the five different parts of prayer. The prayer time will be spontaneous—feel free to offer a prayer, a psalm or other Scripture passage, or a testimony offered as prayer. If there is silence, don't attempt to fill it. God often meets us in the quiet.

The leader will begin each segment with an open-ended sentence ("Lord, we worship You . . ."), and the group will fill in as God draws you through prayer.

▶ "Lord, we worship You . . ."
▶ "Lord, we pray for Your kingdom to come . . ."
▶ "Lord, we pray for Your provision in our lives . . ."
▶ "Lord, we confess our need for Your forgiveness . . ."
▶ "Lord, we ask Your protection as we deal with . . ."

Assignment   10 minutes

Decide which of the following homework electives you will do. Make sure that your choices are reasonable and will be performed by everyone prior to the next meeting.

Elective 1: Reflection—Continue working in your journal. Consider writing a prayer (in any form—poetry, prose, like a psalm, a letter, etc.) each day to God.

Elective 2: Project—Put the names of the group members into a bowl, and have every person draw one name. These will be "prayer partners" for the coming week(s). Consider:

- ▶ setting aside a time each day to pray for your partner
- ▶ sending your partner a note of encouragement, or calling him or her
- ▶ asking your partner how you can pray for him or her

▼ ▼ ▼ ▼ ▼ ▼ ▼ ▼ ▼ ▼ ▼ ▼ ▼ ▼ ▼ ▼ ▼ ▼ ▼ ▼

Reference Notes

Setting: This version of the Lord's Prayer differs from what many churches pray in worship and what is found in Matthew 6:9-13. These differences highlight that it is not so much that the same form must be repeated endlessly (although Jesus does suggest in this passage that this form of prayer should be used), but that one's heart and a desire to communicate matter.

And lead us not into temptation: This request seems to imply that God can lead us into temptation. But James 1 suggests otherwise. The intent of this phrase is that we ask God to protect us from falling away from Him, especially during times of trial (see Matthew's "but deliver us from the evil one").

the man's persistence: The parable of verses 5-13 suggests that God rewards boldness, persistence, and desire. He always acts consistently with His character and will give what is good to us.

the Holy Spirit: The context of this phrase "the Holy Spirit" is so subtle that its message is easy to miss. Readers are tempted to think of this passage as: "If you then, though you are evil, know how to give good gifts to your children, how much more will your Father in heaven give *good gifts* to those who ask Him!" But this passage does not mention "good gifts," it mentions the Spirit of God. This suggests that the greatest gift we can receive from God—and where our prayer should focus—is God Himself.

Additional Resources:

1. Bounds, E. M. *The Power of Prayer.* (and others in his series) Grand Rapids, Mich.: Baker, 1979.

2. Foster, Richard. *Prayer: Finding the Heart's True Home.* San Francisco, Calif.: HarperSanFrancisco, 1992.

3. Eugene Peterson. *Earth and Altar: The Community of Prayer in a Self-Bound Society.* Downers Grove, Ill.: InterVarsity, 1985.

4. Dudley Delffs. *The Prayer-Centered Life.* Colorado Springs, Colo.: NavPress, 1996.

Food for Thought

"Prayer is political action. Prayer is social energy. Prayer is public good. Far more of our nation's life is shaped by prayer than is formed by legislation. That we have not collapsed into anarchy is due more to prayer than to the police. Prayer is a sustained and intricate act of patriotism in the largest sense of that word—far more precise and loving and preserving than any patriotism served up in slogans. That society continues to be livable and that hope continues to be resurgent are attributable to prayer far more than to business prosperity or a flourishing of the arts. The single most important act contributing to whatever health and strength there is in our land is prayer. Not the only thing of course, for God uses all things in his sovereign will . . . but prayer is, all the same, the source action."

—Eugene Peterson,
*Earth and Altar: The Community of Prayer
in a Self-Bound Society,*
p. 15.

Empowering Others

▼▼▼ ▼▼▼▼▼▼▼ ▼▼▼▼▼▼ ▼▼ ▼▼
Overview   10 minutes

❶ *Allow several group members to share what they learned from their homework or to recap what they learned from the last session.*
Then ask someone to read aloud this story and the objectives that follow:

"I wish our church members took their faith more seriously—they don't seem to care!"
Have you ever uttered these words? I have! I used to look to others in my church for help and they were not there for me. I observed the twenty percent who do all the work volunteering for yet another committee or Sunday school assignment. But where was the other eighty percent?
The answer to these questions may be surprising. The problem was me. Trained in the American church to be a leader, I perceived myself as a need-meeter. I arranged my ministry to meet needs. I answered the calls. I responded to complaints. I unknowingly fostered a consumer culture, the very thing I despised. Here is what my leadership looked like:

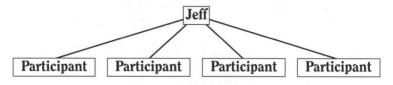

71

I have been challenged to become a structure-builder. My priorities have changed for the good of those I serve. While continuing to meet needs, I have set aside a portion of ministry time to develop leaders. When I get a phone call for help, I make one more call before responding so that I can include others in the helping process. I have developed close "discipleship" relationships which feed my soul and model healthy community to the body of Christ. This is what my ministry now looks like:

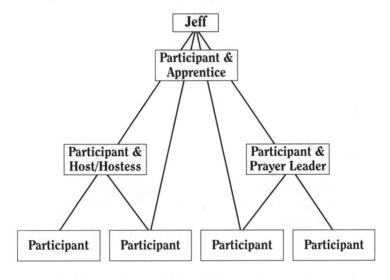

It may look as though I have taken on more responsibility, but in fact I have much more help. In any given small group, I have delegated responsibilities such as leading worship or planning fun times to others. In any given committee, I have equipped other committee members not just to do tasks but to lead in significant areas. A leader who empowers others in this way will have a far greater impact than one who simply meets every need. Leaders who nurture leaders multiply their effectiveness.

In this session we will:

▶ learn about empowering others
▶ examine a portion of Scripture that demonstrates God's ability to give up control
▶ begin to identify potential leaders from within our groups

▼ ▼ ▼ ▼ ▼ ▼ ▼ ▼ ▼ ▼ ▼ ▼ ▼ ▼ ▼ ▼ ▼ ▼ ▼
Beginning   15 minutes

❶ *Question 1 involves creating a role play. In order to
succeed, a role play needs to be played with enthusiasm. If
your role play begins to "fizzle," your group might consider
discussing why you assigned the roles you did for this activity.*

1. We will call this role-play activity, "Out of Character." You
   are members of a small group discussing two ideas. One is
   a fellowship idea that has been proposed by a member:
   rock climbing at Suicide Gulch. The other idea involves
   mission: A member has proposed a one-day visit to a nurs-
   ing home. There are some who feel each idea has merit
   and some who would rather do other activities or nothing.

   Your assignment is to discuss the two ideas while play-
   ing a role that is chosen for you.

   Choose a character from those listed below for each
   group member. The role you play must be the one that the
   group agrees is most unlike you (for example, give a risk-
   oriented person either "Timid Ted/Terri" or "Compassionate
   Cal/Cara"). The characters are identified by statements that
   appear often in their conversation.

   ❏ Character #1—Risky Ralph/Reba: "Come on, that's
     tame! I say go for the gusto. . . ."
   ❏ Character #2—Timid Ted/Terri: "Are you sure nobody's
     going to get hurt? . . ."
   ❏ Character #3—Bossy Bob/Betty: "Come on, people!
     Why can't we all agree on one thing? . . ."
   ❏ Character #4—Compassionate Cal/Cara: "I hear what
     you're saying and I value that. . . ."
   ❏ Character #5—Focused Fred/Fran: "We're getting off
     track. We've got a decision to make. . . ."
   ❏ Character #6—Shy Sam/Sara: "I don't really have
     much to contribute to this conversation. I could do
     whatever the group decides. . . ."

Role play teaches us several things. First, we learn to identify
the parts we play in group life. Second, when we try on a different role we can step outside of ourselves to learn new ways of
interacting. Third, we are challenged to take the edge off of those

parts of our roles that are pronounced (for example, a quiet person may talk more while a talkative person learns to listen).

2. Process the role play by discussing:

    a. What did people learn about themselves by playing their opposites?

    b. If you could use one word to describe the contribution that each member brings to your group, what would it be? (Have the individual being discussed sit silently while each of the other people offers a word.)

3. Every person in a group brings a unique, positive contribution to that group. Learning to affirm a person's place not only creates positive leadership in others, it also defuses potential negative contributions to the group.

    a. What are some ways that individuals in this (or another) small group have encouraged you to practice your gifts?

    b. What are some ways that groups might better encourage people to assume positive roles in a group's life and ministry?

▼ ▼ ▼ ▼ ▼ ▼ ▼ ▼ ▼ ▼ ▼ ▼ ▼ ▼ ▼ ▼ ▼ ▼
Worship   10 minutes—Optional

See the worship section in the appendix for ideas. Since this session is about networking, you might consider using a scripture (such as 1 Corinthians 12) which emphasizes "body life" and spiritual gifts.

The Text ▼▼▼▼▼▼▼▼▼▼▼▼▼▼▼▼ 5 minutes

Many Christians, having tasted God's salvation, can partially understand what it means to be "saved." But God does not stop there—He elevates us to the position of sonship and daughtership; He forgives all our sins; and He shares His plan with us and allows us to work toward its fulfillment. In Ephesians 1 we can see both the heart of God (to share) and God's leadership style (to freely give blessing and authority). By learning from God we can develop our own call to empower others for ministry.

❶ *Have someone read the text aloud. You may also read some or all of the reference notes on page 80.*

Praise be to the God and Father of our Lord Jesus Christ, **who has blessed us** in the heavenly realms with every spiritual blessing in Christ. For he chose us in him before the creation of the world to be holy and blameless in his sight. In love he predestined us to be adopted as his sons through Jesus Christ, in accordance with his pleasure and will—**to the praise of his glorious grace,** which he has freely given us in the One he loves. In him we have **redemption** through his blood, the forgiveness of sins, in accordance with the riches of God's grace that he lavished on us with all wisdom and understanding. And he made known to us the **mystery of his will** according to his good pleasure, which he purposed in Christ, to be put into effect when the times will have reached their fulfillment—to bring all things in heaven and on earth together under one head, even Christ.

In him we were also chosen, having been predestined according to the plan of him who works out everything in conformity with the purpose of his will, in order that we, who were the first to hope in Christ, might be for the praise of his glory. And you also were included in Christ when you heard the word of truth, the gospel of your salvation. Having believed, you were marked in him with a seal, the promised Holy Spirit, who is **a deposit** guaranteeing our inheritance until the redemption of those who are God's possession—to the praise of his glory.

(Ephesians 1:3-14)

4. What does it mean that God blesses us:

    ❐ "in the heavenly realms"?
    ❐ "with every spiritual blessing in Christ"?

5. This passage lists six blessings that belong to every Christian. These blessings appear in logical or chronological order regarding their application in the lives of Christians.

    ❐ God chose us to be set apart and pure in His sight.
    ❐ God adopted us to be His sons and daughters.
    ❐ God redeemed (purchased) us so that He might lavish us with grace.
    ❐ God has revealed His will to us and continues to do so.
    ❐ God chose us to share in His praise and glory.
    ❐ God gave us the Holy Spirit to ensure future promises.

    For each of these blessings, answer two questions:

    a. What does a Christian receive in this blessing?

    b. How does this blessing affect a Christian's life now?

6. When you consider the alternatives available to God in His dealings with humans (He could have consigned us to hell; or forgiven but not forgotten; or ignored our sin and pretended we were perfect), this passage has much to teach about who God is and how God acts toward His followers. Identify at least three or four things we can learn about God from this passage. What word(s) or sentence best summarizes your discoveries?

Applying the Text   15 minutes

7. It is up to us to choose to empower others just as God
    empowers us. We would not be leaders in the church, and
    there would be no church, if God was unable to "let go" and
    allow others to serve. As God allows us to serve, give, and
    lead, so we are called to equip others to do the same. But
    there is more to empowering others than just giving. We
    have to know how and when to give leadership to a person.

    a. Which of the following is closest to the best way to give
       leadership away?

       ❏ Jim hoards leadership because nobody can do it right.
       ❏ Sarah assigns jobs to everybody.
       ❏ Tim has one apprentice who shares all leadership
         with him.
       ❏ Jan can't wait to share leadership with her small
         group members.
       ❏ Ted systematically works his way out of a job every
         time he leads a group.

    b. What are potential deficiencies in each of the ways
       listed above?

Healthy leaders learn a four-step process for sharing leadership:

    ▶ Step 1—Consult: "What do you think?"
    ▶ Step 2—Probe: "What would you do?"
    ▶ Step 3—Ask: "How would you like to do this?"
    ▶ Step 4—Evaluate: "What have you learned from
              doing this?"

8. Based on those four steps, discuss how a good leader might first identify the gifts of the following people, and then give them an appropriate leadership responsibility:

❏ Shelby is a good listener.
❏ Dana is super-organized.
❏ Mark keeps the group on track.

9. In order to empower others effectively, leaders must deal with their own insecurities. Which of the following (there may be more than one) are true of you?

❏ It is easier to do the job myself.
❏ Others don't do the work as well as I would.
❏ It takes too much time to develop leaders.
❏ I worry that people will think I am shirking my responsibilities if I get others to do the work.
❏ I am concerned about the time stresses that leadership demands may make on others.

10. What can you do to address (and overcome) these hangups?

▼ ▼ ▼ ▼ ▼ ▼ ▼ ▼ ▼ ▼ ▼ ▼ ▼ ▼ ▼ ▼ ▼ ▼
Assignment 10 minutes

Decide which of the following homework electives you will do. Make sure that your choices are reasonable and will be performed by everyone prior to the next meeting.

Elective 1: Reflection—There are two issues to consider in your journal. First is the extent to which you are willing to give leadership away. As you reflect on your leadership style, consider several things:

► How do I "come across" as a leader? Do I allow others to perform significant roles and duties according to their abilities? Why or why not?

► What words would I (and do others) use to identify my leadership style? What aspects of my style empower others? What aspects of my style keep others from serving as they might?

The second issue is to begin identifying the leadership abilities of those who are in the group(s) you lead so that you can begin empowering them.

▶ Names of those who are in my group(s) that I lead
▶ Positive and negative group contributions for each
▶ Ways I can encourage group members to take larger roles and responsibilities

Elective 2: Project—Within the next few weeks, if you have opportunity to lead, fill out this mini-questionnaire. Also, ask another person who was present to complete it.

On a scale of 0 to 5, rank how you behaved at this leadership event in each of these categories:

0	1	2	3	4	5
Didn't talk enough				Talked too much	

0	1	2	3	4	5
Didn't listen to others				Valued others' advice	

0	1	2	3	4	5
Did all the work myself				Allowed others to help significantly	

0	1	2	3	4	5
Need to develop leaders				Am developing leaders	

0	1	2	3	4	5
Have no plan				Have a long-term plan	

▼▼▼▼▼▼▼▼▼▼▼▼▼▼▼▼▼▼
Prayer   10 minutes

Stand in a circle. Complete this statement for the person on your right: "One thing I have learned about you from being in this group is. . . ." Let each person pray aloud, beginning with the leader. Thank God for what you are learning, and pray that God's work will deepen. If you would rather pray silently, please say "Amen" aloud to let the others know you are finished.

▼ ▼
Reference Notes

Setting: Ephesians 1:3-14, while doctrinal in content, is in the form of a thanksgiving and prayer. Paul seems to trip over himself in his exuberance as insight into God forms itself into praise and worship. In fact, these twelve verses are one very long, complex sentence. The focus of the passage is on God and what He has done for us through Jesus Christ.

who has blessed us: This phrase, set in the Greek aorist tense, refers to the fact that our blessing is not a future event, but has already happened. Our benefits in God are to be claimed now.

to the praise of his glorious grace: There are two motives mentioned in these verses for God's call and adoption: love (verse 4) and God's glory (verse 6). In relation to His glory, we know from Scripture that only through God is there salvation and abundant life. So God's plan is to reveal God's glory so that we, having tasted His love, might experience all of His blessings.

redemption: The Greek word refers to release from captivity. The Greek word for "forgiveness" involves a similar idea: release from something that binds a person. In this context, Jesus' blood sets us free from our sins.

mystery of his will: This term refers to God's making clear something that was not clear before—in this case, that the Messiah has come in the flesh and God will bring all things together under the rule of Christ. We share in this plan as Christians!

a deposit: When a loan is made, something valuable is given to guarantee payment. So the Holy Spirit has become God's "loan guarantee" that everything we have now and hope to receive in Him will be "made good."

Provocative Teaching

▼ ▼ ▼ ▼ ▼ ▼ ▼ ▼ ▼ ▼ ▼ ▼ ▼ ▼ ▼ ▼ ▼
Overview   10 minutes

❶ *Allow several group members to share what they learned from their homework or recap what they learned from the last session.*

Then ask someone to read aloud these thoughts and the objectives that follow.

Some lay leaders may panic when they read the title to this session. I can hear them say, "What?! Me a teacher? No way! I'll lead, but I won't teach!"

The idea of being a teacher was not one that I took upon myself naturally. I had too many preconceptions of teaching, most of which involved my most excruciating experiences as a learner. I pictured faces of students enduring blobs of boredom pouring forth from a glassy-eyed nonperson. It was too much for me.

Then I ran into the verses about Jesus, that He "taught as one who had authority, and not as their teachers of the law." What did this mean—that Jesus taught, yet was interesting? That His speaking was provocative, challenging, irresistible, penetrating? I have revisited the idea that teaching can be provocative, rather than merely the rote downloading of information.

Most leaders using this resource are involved in small groups, Sunday school, children's ministry, or youth ministry. Trained according to "facilitative leadership" techniques, you may have learned to avoid the word "teacher." It has been replaced with concepts like partnership, teamwork, and shared learning. Many leaders have embraced the idea that "anyone can do this."

But there is more to leading than just letting students learn. Teachers are models who (consciously or unconsciously) affect learners in many subtle and indirect ways. They are facilitators who teach learners how to engage in directed interaction. They are instructors who find things that are not obvious, who direct minds in directions they may not want to go, who call forth behaviors that have never been considered.

Effective leaders know how to help people learn. They also know how to teach. Their teaching comes in many forms: conversation, life experience, discussion, lecture, object lessons, and more. Their guidance provokes insight.

In this session we will:

> ▶ share what we have learned through our group experience thus far
> ▶ evaluate Jesus' use of a "teachable moment" in the lives of His disciples
> ▶ develop positive principles of teaching
> ▶ evaluate several teaching styles and describe our own

Beginning ▼▼▼▼▼▼▼▼▼▼▼▼▼▼▼▼▼▼▼ 20 minutes

❶ *Go around the room and allow each person to answer the first question.*

1. Who is the most effective teacher you ever had? What made this person such a good teacher?

2. According to your experience and preferences, develop (as a group) five things that effective teachers do.

The Text   5 minutes

Good teachers are able to convey ideas through words in a positive manner. Great teachers are able to instruct not just through their words but through their lives and leadership. In John 13, Jesus the Rabbi teaches His disciples through life experience.

❶ *Have someone read the text aloud. You may also read some or all of the reference notes on page 88.*

Just before the Passover Feast, Jesus knew that the time had come to leave this world to go to the Father. Having loved his dear companions, he continued to love them right to the end. It was suppertime. The Devil by now had Judas, son of Simon the Iscariot, firmly in his grasp, all set for the betrayal. **Jesus knew** that **the Father had put him in complete charge of everything, that he came from God** and was on his way back to God. So he got up from the supper table, set aside his robe, and put on an apron. Then he poured water into a basin and began to **wash the feet** of the disciples, drying them with an apron. When he got to Simon Peter, Peter said, "Master, *you* wash *my* feet?"

Jesus answered, "You don't understand now what I'm doing, but it will be clear enough to you later."

Peter persisted, **"You're not going to wash my feet— ever!"**

Jesus said, "If I don't wash you, you can't be part of what I'm doing."

"Master!" said Peter. "Not only my feet, then. Wash my hands! Wash my head!"

Jesus said, "If you've had a bath in the morning, you only need your feet washed now and you're clean from head to toe. My concern, you understand, is holiness, not hygiene. So now you're clean. But not every one of you." (He knew who was betraying him. That's why he said, "Not every one of you.") After he had finished washing their feet, he took his robe, put it back on, and went back to his place at the table.

Then he said, "Do you understand what I have done to you? You address me as 'Teacher' and 'Master,' and rightly so. That is what I am. So if I, the Master and Teacher, washed your feet, you must now wash each other's feet. I've laid down a pattern for you. What I've done, you do. I'm only pointing out the obvious. A servant is not ranked above his master; an employee doesn't give orders to the employer. If you understand what I'm telling you, act like it—and live a blessed life."

(John 13:1-20, MSG)

▼ ▼ ▼ ▼ ▼ ▼ ▼ ▼ ▼ ▼ ▼ ▼ ▼ ▼ ▼ ▼ ▼ ▼ ▼
Understanding the Text   15 minutes

3. Why do you suppose the disciples didn't wash each others' feet?

4. Provocative teachers do not merely dispense information. Their words and actions are the result of a reflective lifestyle. In this passage, Jesus' teaching flows from several issues that He was pondering. Look over these phrases from the first few verses and discuss how they affected His words and actions in this teaching event:

   ❑ Jesus knew that He was leaving this world.
   ❑ Jesus loved His dear companions, and continued to do so to the very end.
   ❑ Jesus knew that the Father had put Him in charge of everything.
   ❑ Jesus knew that He came from God and was returning to God.

5. Examine the exchange between Peter and the Lord.

   a. What was going on in Peter's mind and heart as Jesus approached him?

b. What did Jesus communicate to Peter through their conversation?

6. What were different teaching elements Jesus used in these events?

7. What can we learn about Jesus the teacher from this experience?

▼ ▼ ▼ ▼ ▼ ▼ ▼ ▼ ▼ ▼ ▼ ▼ ▼ ▼ ▼ ▼ ▼ ▼
Applying the Text   20 minutes

8. Many teachers get stuck in a rut of techniques, using the same styles and activities over and over. This predictability detracts from the learning event. Look over the following list of five positive teaching principles:

   ❒ Provocative teaching is transcendent—it calls forth behaviors, thoughts, and actions that students may never have considered or implemented.
   ❒ Provocative teaching is flexible—it adapts to new situations.
   ❒ Provocative teaching is consistent—it follows through on promises.
   ❒ Provocative teaching is thought-provoking—it presents ideas clearly and in such a manner that minds are stimulated to process and go further in learning.
   ❒ Provocative teaching is creative—it finds fun, different, challenging, and positive ways to make a point; and it

addresses people who learn by seeing, by hearing, or by doing.

   a. Choose one of those principles that you follow well. In what ways do you do it?

   b. Choose one at which you are not proficient. What would it take for you to grow in this area?

9. Based on the five principles listed above, evaluate the following teaching styles for their strengths and weaknesses:

☐ "Lecture Len" is intelligent, organized, and coherent. He comes to group prepared and offers tremendous lectures on biblical, theological, and historical issues.

☐ "Creative Catherine" is a fun, "artsy" person. She thinks of creative things for the group to do—so much so that the group finds its time flies by. Although group members interact around projects, there is not much time for conversation or discussion.

☐ "Worried Wendy" is so concerned that she might not know answers that she spends many hours between meetings consulting Bible dictionaries and other resources for both relevant and obscure facts. She comes extremely well prepared to group meetings. At times she gets impatient with group members who question the ideas she has gleaned from her study.

10. Discuss what is next for your group. Since this is a leadership group, most of you have roles in the ministry that are ongoing. Discuss the following options:

☐ Shall we continue? If so, create a covenant. (Page 47 has a sample covenant.)

☐ Shall we end? If so, shall we plan a party? (See Assignment: Project)

☐ Shall we end for now, and pick up in the future? If so, when?

▼▼▼▼▼▼▼▼▼▼▼▼▼▼▼▼▼▼▼▼▼
Assignment
10 minutes

Individuals may decide which of the following homework electives they will do.

Elective 1: Reflection—Continue working in your journal. Reflect on these questions, based on the five principles of positive teaching under question 8 on pages 85 and 86:

- ► For each of the five, which parts do I do well?
- ► For each of the five, what are some things I need to work on?
- ► What are steps I can take to improve in some of the areas that have shown up in my reflection?

Elective 2: Project—As a group, plan an outing or a party for fun.

▼▼▼▼▼▼▼▼▼▼▼▼▼▼▼▼▼▼▼▼▼
Prayer
10 minutes

11. Beginning with the leader and moving from individual to individual in a circle to his or her left, allow group members to finish these two sentences for each person:

    ❑ Something I have learned from you because of our involvement in this group is. . . .
    ❑ Something I appreciate about you because of our involvement in this group is. . . .

Stand in a circle. You may consider completing this sentence in your prayer time: "Lord, as we move on to something new we thank You for. . . ."

▼ ▼ ▼ ▼ ▼ ▼ ▼ ▼ ▼ ▼ ▼ ▼ ▼ ▼ ▼ ▼ ▼ ▼ ▼ ▼
Reference Notes

Setting: The events of this passage occurred the evening before Jesus was to die. The disciples had gathered in the room for the Last Supper, which followed this event.

Jesus knew: This passage is full of statements related to Jesus' self-awareness. He knew it was time to return to God (verse 1); He knew He had all authority (verse 3); He knew He was about to be betrayed (verses 2,11); and He knew who the true disciples were (verse 18). Jesus' knowledge manifested itself not only in His lifestyle, but in His thoughts and teaching as well.

the Father had put him in complete charge of everything, that he came from God: An ironic set of statements in light of the public act of humility that Jesus performed to put on a towel and wash His followers' feet. There is something profound in these words. That is, one who is at rest with his or her place and call is willing to serve. Jesus' self-awareness set Him free from positioning and striving.

wash the feet: In Jesus' day people wore sandals, and their feet got filthy in the streets. It was polite for the servant of a host to wash the dust off guests' feet when they visited. This was normally the job of the lowest household slave, since it was a dirty job and feet were considered the lowliest part of the body. In the case of the Last Supper, the host of the home was not present, so there was a question about who was to wash the others' feet.

"You're not going to wash my feet—ever!": Perhaps humbled by Jesus' actions, Peter attempted his own brand of humility. He emphatically stated that Jesus was not to degrade Himself by cleaning his feet. But Jesus was equally emphatic in His reply: "If I don't wash you, you can't be part of what I'm doing."

How to Prepare for Your Group

Distinctives of a Leadership Group

Groups using this resource will most likely be composed of leaders. There are several possible assumptions under which leader groups may form:

> ▶ long-term leadership support groups that function like small groups

> ▶ short-term (seven-session) leadership support groups that meet for an abbreviated period of time (every week for seven weeks; once a month for seven months) for ongoing support and training

> ▶ ongoing leadership training groups that use resources like this one for training material

> ▶ occasional short-term leadership support groups that meet for abbreviated studies (seven sessions), then re-form in the next year for another short-term experience

Optimum Size of the Group

Group size is optimum or maximum when it matches the leader's (and apprentice leader's) ability to care adequately for the group members. There is no magic number, but it is generally accepted that the average lay leader can adequately care for around five or six people. Therefore, a leader with an apprentice can lead a group of around ten to twelve in regular attendance. Once the group gets larger than that on a regular basis, group dynamics change and the dominant personalities will tend to control the discussion and sharing times.

If you find yourself in a group that has grown large, you can still offer a comfortable place for people to share their lives and prayers if you will ask them to break down into groups of three to four (never more than five) for discussion and prayer. Check with the host or hostess for separate areas of the house where subgroups may go for ease of hearing and confidentiality.

Room Setup

Room setup is a large factor in determining the friendliness of a meeting. Consider these questions:

- ▶ Can the room be set up so that everyone is facing each other?

- ▶ Is the room large enough to accommodate ten to twelve people comfortably?

- ▶ Can everyone in the room make eye contact? (It is important that everyone is face to face, not in the second row or in back of another participant.)

- ▶ Is the room free from distractions?

A Successful First Meeting: Pray, Play, Recruit

The first meeting often sets the pace for the group, so it is very important.

Your most important job is to pray and remind yourself that you are in partnership with God. As you are connected with Him in prayer and are refreshed by Him, you will have something significant to offer the group.

Next, relax. You probably have much higher expectations and greater demands on yourself than anyone else in the group.

Prepare. Know what you intend to do, and in a general sense, what you want to convey to the group. However, don't get caught in the trap of having a rigid agenda.

Spend some time with your host or hostess ahead of time. Find out what his or her expectations are, and share your general agenda and time schedule. Determine what the hosts are comfortable with concerning how late group members may stay, any off-limit areas of the home, and so on. If you set some house rules for the group, or ask the host to do so, you will head off possible misunderstandings and problems later on.

Recruit leaders to attend your group. If your group is based in a church, you might invite small group leaders, Sunday school teachers, church board members, worship leaders, and even church staff. On the other hand, this guide is also effective for ministry teams and gatherings of leaders who are not based in one church. Be upbeat about the possibilities offered by the group. Make a list of people to invite. Pray for those on your list, and then invite them. An answer of "I don't know" or "maybe" is not a "no." Often people need some time to think about or to digest the idea. Give them a few days or a week, and extend the invitation again.

Finally, remember that God wants you to succeed in leading this group, and He loves these people more than you do. Prepare, pray, and then go in His strength and the confidence you have in His ability to mold you into a loving group.

▼▼▼▼▼▼▼▼▼▼▼▼▼ ▼ ▼ ▼ ▼ ▼
FACILITATING WORSHIP IN THE SMALL GROUP

The small group offers an environment where people can learn to worship God while also learning to interact with other worshipers. The key issues in leading worship in a group are: turning our thoughts and attention totally to God; being honest; and letting God know how much we love and adore Him for who He is. If people are encouraged and led (not driven) into worship, they will grow in confidence and ability. They will learn the delicate balance between focusing on God and being aware of other worshipers. These skills, which can help you maintain balance and order, can then be used in the congregational setting as well as in private worship.

To relieve pressure on your time, you could assign your apprentice or someone else in the group the task of planning worship for each meeting.

Using the Psalms for Personal and Group Worship

The Psalms are a beautiful and personal collection of the very heartbeat of King David and other psalmists. Eugene Peterson's rendering of the Psalms in *The Message* is down-to-earth and allows you to experience the emotions of the author. The Psalms stir our hearts, making us more vulnerable to God and leading us into more intimate communication with Him.

Read a section of the Psalms. Take time to meditate on that

section and then on each verse. Let the tone, the emotion, the intensity, and the intimacy expressed by the author influence your thinking and touch your heart.

Try varying the way in which you read the psalm. You could have someone read one verse at a time, pausing between verses to allow the group to think about each verse silently. You could read the psalm in unison, or have each half of the group read the verses alternately.

A Cappella Singing as Worship

If no one plays an instrument, the group may sing a cappella (without instruments). There should be one person who leads, initiates, and determines the direction and duration of worship through song. In rare instances, a group may allow various individuals to initiate songs at random, with the group joining in spontaneously. The risk in this is that the group may end up singing the old favorites of the most vocal person, rather than a flow of worship led by the Spirit of God. It is very important that the leader is wise and gentle, able to discern and guide through the possible pitfalls of this approach.

Using a Guitar, Piano, Portable Keyboard, or Recording to Lead Worship in Song

The worship leader does not have to play an instrument but should be the one who selects, begins, and ends the songs. When possible, there should be a person who plays an instrument (such as guitar or keyboard) and who also sings. He or she may be accompanied by other players and singers as necessary and appropriate. The worship leader also needs to work closely with the group leader to coordinate with the leader's plans for the group, and to adjust the length of worship (and even the mood if necessary) to complement the group agenda. In many groups where a worship leader is active, the worship leader is seen as part of the group leadership team.

When choosing songs for group worship, attention should be given to a flow in the songs. Worship is often broken into two parts: Worship songs which focus on who God is, and Praise songs which focus on what God does. These two forms of worship can also be subdivided into first-person songs (those spoken directly to Jesus, God the Father, and the Holy Spirit), and third person songs (those sung about God, His attributes, and what He has done).

Many groups have success with prerecorded worship songs.

Many are available today. The important thing is to create an environment of worship and surrender to God, no matter what musical means are employed.

Using Silence and Meditation as Worship

It is important to use silence and meditation as part of your group worship. The selah or pause that is injected throughout the Psalms is a good cue for us to take a few moments and quietly reflect. Meditation (being silent and thinking about what you have just read or heard) is good for the group, and a discipline that we do not practice enough.

Reading or Quoting Favorite Scriptures

Scripture reading can be effective in directing the group's attention to God and His desire to be in communion with us. When busy people hear the Word proclaimed and are encouraged to meditate on it, their attention and focus can be directed from their circumstances to our awesome and holy God!

▼ ▼ ▼ ▼ ▼ ▼ ▼ ▼ ▼ ▼ ▼ ▼ ▼ ▼ ▼ ▼ ▼ ▼ ▼ ▼
RECRUITING AN APPRENTICE

One of the ideal uses for this guide is the training of apprentice leaders. Apprentices are the key to sustainable growth in a small-group system.

Why Have an Apprentice?

God's plan is to call all men and women and ask everyone to put their hand to the plow: "Jesus said, 'No procrastination. No backward looks. You can't put God's kingdom off till tomorrow. Seize the day'" (Luke 9:62, MSG).

Two things in the life of a healthy small group are necessary and predictable. One is that the group will attract and add new members. As the members begin to take ownership of the group, they will want to invite friends, fellow workers, fellow churchgoers, and family members to come and see what's happening. Consequently, the small group will grow and eventually become a large group. However, an effective group should not grow much past ten or twelve regular attendees. We know that an average layperson leading a group will be able to adequately care for around five people, so with a group of ten there are already people falling through the cracks of care and follow-up. Therefore, the second necessary fact of group life has already come into play: leadership multiplication, or what is currently termed "apprentice leader development." It is a natural component of life to grow, multiply, and grow some more. Such is the case with normal, healthy small groups—they grow, multiply into two groups, and the two continue to grow.

If your group is to follow this natural course, it only makes sense to plan for it and participate in the process. Planning should encompass several questions:

- ► Who can lead?
- ► How do I recruit someone?
- ► How soon do I recruit an apprentice?
- ► How do I begin developing this person into a leader?

Whom to Recruit

Apprentice-making is not a random, mechanical action, but is best worked out through prayer and wise counsel. Check with your pastor and/or small group coordinator. Get some help in selecting a person who is interested in serving and praying for other members of the group. Leadership is never lording over others or just showing up and directing a meeting. Instead, it fulfills God's plan for all His sons and daughters to be cared for and assisted along the way toward Him. The best leaders are generally the best servants. Look for the persons who enjoy serving and helping. Look for people who have:

- ► a searching mind
- ► a humble heart
- ► an evident gift
- ► a faithful spirit

Spend time with them. Fan their fire. People are already motivated by God—tap into that!

- ► Tell them your vision of their potential.
- ► Share your commitment to their development.
- ► Provide them with a specific assignment. "He who is faithful with little things will be faithful in big things."
- ► Let them pray about the opportunity.
- ► If they say yes, give them a job description and involve them in ministry.[1]

► If they say no, observe them for a while and approach them again.

When recruiting apprentice leaders, watch for "Davids"—people who at first glance are not obvious leaders. Our propensity is to look for the person who is naturally talented or a manager in business. This has always been the way leaders and followers have leaned in looking for and choosing someone to lead them. God knew this and intervened through the prophet Samuel when he was sent to single out and anoint the next king:

> But the LORD said to Samuel, "Do not consider his appearance or his height, for I have rejected him." The LORD does not look at the things man looks at. Man looks at the outward appearance, but the LORD looks at the heart.
>
> (1 Samuel 16:7)

This amazing act of divine intervention expressed God's wisdom and compassion. God knew even Samuel would tend to go to the eldest, best-looking son. But God had Samuel look at each of the sons and hear God say "not this one," until David was sent for and received the Lord's approval.

Jesus also gave us direction and guidelines to follow in selecting leaders and apprentices. He said the people were like sheep without a shepherd (Matthew 9:36) and commanded His disciples to pray for workers for the harvest. The disciples were the answer to the prayer. The call to the disciples is the call to us, and Jesus' model is instructive. He started with them as workers. They were not hired; they were developed and empowered. Only after several years were they released and deployed as leaders.

Raising up apprentice leaders will be messy and difficult. It takes time, energy, and resources, somewhat like training little children. They are interested, exuberant, and sometimes motivated. But often in attempting to do a task for the first time, they miss the mark and get discouraged. We have an awesome opportunity and responsibility to remind them that failure is always a step in the right direction, if we learn from it. No one does it all right on the first try, so don't wait for perfection until you praise them. Praise any right step toward the goal.

---

1. *The Small Group Fitness Kit,* by Thom Corrigan (NavPress, 1996), gives a sample job description for an apprentice leader.

Turn your group into a community.

Most study guides are designed for individual use. While packed with good material, they don't provide much help in the way of group dynamic.

That's where PILGRIMAGE study guides are different. By incorporating community-building questions and exercises into each session, PILGRIMAGE guides will help your group grow closer relationally as you grow deeper spiritually. THE PILGRIMAGE SERIES includes titles like:

Seven Traits of a Successful Leader
by Jeff Arnold
Whether you're teaching a class or leading a group, there are certain character qualities that can significantly increase your impact. This guide will help you develop the seven essential traits of a successful leader.
(ISBN: 1-57683-019-5; 7 sessions; 96 pages)

Experiencing Community
by Thom Corrigan
Whether you're forming a new group or would like to build a stronger bond of community in your existing group, this seven-week study is the perfect "body-builder."
(ISBN: 8-09109-938-7; 7 sessions; 80 pages)

What We Believe
by Jeff Arnold
Of all the doctrines and versions of Christianity in circulation today, which ones are non-negotiable? Drawn from the Apostles' Creed, *What We Believe* examines the age old core beliefs of the Faith.
(ISBN: 1-57683-071-3; 8 sessions; 80 pages)

101 Great Ideas to Create a Caring Group
by Thom Corrigan
Many believe the single highest felt need in our society is the need to belong. To know someone else cares about us. Here are 101 tried and true ideas for cultivating an atmosphere of care in any small group.
(ISBN: 1-57683-072-1; 80 pages)

These and other NavPress study guides are available at your local Christian bookstore. Or call 1-800-366-7788 to order.

NAVPRESS
BRINGING TRUTH TO LIFE